Southern cultures

Volume 4, Number 2
Published by the
University of North Carolina Press
for the
Center for the Study of the American South
at the University of North Carolina at Chapel Hill

front porch

"Identity" is a big deal these days. A quick check of the Internet reveals three categories and 540 separate Web sites containing the keyword "identity." Contrary to what university-based identity watchers might think, most of them have to do with corporate identity. It seems there are lots of unidentified businesses out there, all in need of other businesses who can set them up with corporate logos, Web sites, direct mail, print advertising, product design, and everything else an up-to-date identity requires. And if you need to change your business identity, the corporate identifiers can fix you right up with the necessary changes to all of the above. If anyone ever doubted the constructed nature of identity, here's the proof. The rest of the Internet's "identity" entries are a good deal more earnest. The obvious assortment of ethnic identities are up for discussion: Indian American (not the same as Native American), Jewish, Australian, Asian American, African American female, biracial, "Mexican—Not Latino—Not Hispanic," even Breton. There are discussions of gender identity, sexual identity, dissociative identity disorder, and the real identities of Jesus and Shakespeare. There is also one Web

above: *Courtesy of Auburn University Department of Archives and Manuscripts.*

site described as "the only page ever needed for a man struggling to find his true identity," which takes its philosophical cue from the teachings of Conan the Barbarian. Really.

The typical explanations for all this current interest in identity usually invoke the impersonality of modern life, the need to claim something unique, personal, and authentic in the face of anonymous, media-driven mass culture, and, as often as not, a deep-seated grievance against past attempts—often quite successful—to ridicule, marginalize, penalize, or repress some distinctive aspect of personal or group identity.

Southerners are well aware of the celebrative and punitive aspects of group identity. Most any southerner can tell you about some time or another when he or she felt labeled with an unwelcome stereotype, and felt the urge to deny that southernness could be summed up in any particular trait or image. Without batting an eye at the contradiction, many of us are just as ready to complete the sentence "all southerners are ———" with any number of complimentary words and phrases. Even if we resist the urge to typecast, we're all familiar with the images that southerners and nonsoutherners alike resort to in tales about southern identity: poor, dumb, bigoted, aristocratic, violent, polite. Scarlett O'Hara and the Beverly Hillbillies. Uncle Remus and Preacher Nat. NASCAR races and the debutante ball.

To face the truth squarely, it would be hard to argue that *Southern Cultures* is not part of the South's cult of regional identity. Chewing over various facets of being southern seems to be what our authors do best. And why not? Given the obvious power of the identity question to rivet modern attention, there doesn't seem to be any likelihood that people will give up dwelling on this subject for something else. Under the circumstances, skeptical and reflective explorations of the identity question look like a big improvement over some of the uglier forms of identity politics we see out there, from Bosnia to places nearer by. Certainly the authors in this issue take that approach, and we hope you enjoy their musings as much as we have.

Two enduring stereotypes of southern female identity are the "Lady" and the "Sharecropper." The lady is famous from her starring role in a thousand movies and plantation romances. She is beautiful, graceful, courteous, charitable, and charming; she is as well bred on the outside as a chest full of family silver and as steely inside as Uncle Beauregard's cavalry sword. The female sharecropper stares at us from numerous WPA photographs: gaunt, haggard, beaten down with suffering, hardened with toil and ignorance, everybody's favorite victim.

Can the identities of "lady" and "sharecropper" go together? The stereotypes say "no," but Elizabeth Payne's study of the life of a spirited and successful union organizer in 1930s Arkansas indicates otherwise. Myrtle Lawrence, a sharecropper who joined the Southern Tenant Farmers' Union (STFU) in 1936, used her talents to bring whites and blacks of the Arkansas Delta together against the economic hardship of the depths of the Great Depression. Her success at bringing others into the STFU was recognized by the union's leaders, but their image of her, based on stereotypes derived from Tobacco Road and Dorothea Lange photographs, drove them to downplay her visibility and influence within the union. Focusing primarily on her penchant for snuff, brazen style, and double negatives, they felt that she would offend northern liberals, the movement's primary supporters. Payne details here, and in a forthcoming book, how Lawrence's true identity as an honest, hard-working, and gracious woman (a "lady" in the eyes of those close to her) diginified her life and reminds us that too much emphasis on identity can slow the pace of social change.

Celeste Ray explores a different kind of identity in her discussion of the Scottish heritage movement. She tells us that the South is home to an enthusiastic circle of folks who celebrate their Scottish heritage, real or imagined. Not only are Highland games festivals growing in popularity, but the participants are eager to connect their ideas about things Scottish with their ideas about the South. There are women in plaid hoopskirts, Confederate versions of Scottish tartans, and overlapping stories of southern and Scottish lost causes. What is the meaning of all this? How much is real and how much of this "heritage" is imaginary? Why are so many white southerners so eager to discover and display their Scottish roots? Ray discovers that the heritage movement has a lot to do with bringing unpopular aspects of southern identity back inside the circle of contemporary legitimacy.

Speaking of identity, who was the real Thomas Jefferson? Does it matter? The Sage of Monticello has always received a share of bad press, as well as national and regional adulation. Everyone can find the Jefferson he or she is looking for: the democrat, the aristocrat, the slaveholder, the statesman, the demagogue, the philosopher, the racist. Recent books about Jefferson, particularly those by Conor Cruise O'Brien and Annette Gordon-Reed, have revived some of the old controversies. Was Jefferson's self-righteousness responsible for more harm than good in American life and culture? More specifically, what was the nature of his alleged relationship with the slave woman Sally Hemings? Was she his concubine? Were they lovers? Does it matter? Is there any valid connection between the character of Thomas Jefferson and the character of the rest of us?

Robert McDonald does not attempt to solve these mysteries, but he raises questions about the questions. Specifically, he asks what the charges about Jefferson's sex life have done to the Sage's reputation over the years. In the beginning, at least, it did not seem to matter if the accusations about Jefferson and Hemings were true or not. The president's enemies hated him as much as ever and his friends did not seem to care. The identity of Thomas Jefferson seemed unshakable in the minds of his contemporaries, regardless of what they said about him in the newspapers. Why was this so? Was there something about the idea of Jefferson the concubine-keeper that actually appealed to his potential supporters? McDonald discusses these aspects of the ancient controversy as an unexplored dimension of the enduring identity crisis of America's most enigmatic Founder.

Our shorter features offer a zesty mix of the new and the traditional. Poet Michael Chitwood was forcefully struck by one of our earlier articles, the story of how author T. H. Breen rediscovered the Great Wagon Road of upland North Carolina. He shared his response with us in the form of a poem, which we share in turn with our readers. Our music section, "Up Beat Down South," brings in guest author Patrick Huber to discuss some of the songs of one of the South's epic labor struggles, the great Gastonia textile strike of 1929. We have an especially rich book review section this time, and our food section raises a question of southern identity all its own: "How German is southern cooking?" Finally, Lauren F. Winner shares with us some of the most disturbing aspects of southern identity in her "Not Forgotten" discussion of a summer program for suburban middle-schoolers. In this case, "Not Forgotten" is a glaring misnomer, for these children (and especially those who have taught them) seem to have forgotten a lot. How much should they remember? Who should teach them? In the future, how much reality will a southern identity based on ancient grievance have for the children of privilege? Winner leaves us with important questions to ponder.

On a lighter note, I should also report that the Internet contains 426 categories and 17,983 Web sites containing the keyword "South." These range, of course, from South Korea to South Dakota, with stops in South Ayreshire and New South Wales. Even so, there seems to be at least as much interest out there in the "South" as there is in "identity," and that doesn't seem likely to change very soon. So make the most of it. Curl up with a "Big O" and interrogate our identity constructions with another big issue of *Southern Cultures*.

HARRY WATSON, *Coeditor*

The Lady Was a Sharecropper
Myrtle Lawrence and the
Southern Tenant Farmers' Union

by Elizabeth Anne Payne

with photographs by Louise Boyle

Myrtle Lawrence shells peas in her dining room with (left to right) granddaughter Lucille Kimbrell, daughter Icy Jewel Lawrence, and grandson Elroe Kimbrell. Photograph by Louise Boyle. Courtesy of the Kheel Center for Labor-Management Documentation & Archives, Cornell University.

Editors' note: This essay is part of a forthcoming book, *"Showers of Blessings": Myrtle Lawrence and the Southern Tenant Farmers' Union.*

rom his deathbed, Alabama native Aubrey Williams pleaded for a more textured understanding of the South's poor whites. Lamenting that the poor white southerner "has been despised and insulted over and over, and he has been cheated and he has been gulled and he has been exploited," Williams hoped to share his hard-earned wisdom that the struggle of the African American was entwined intrinsically with the fate of the southern poor white. As a New Deal administrator, the director of the National Youth Administration, and an activist in numerous reform organizations, Williams had lived his life serving the southern poor of both races. The "cause of the Negro cannot be won," he insisted. "The South cannot be saved until he [the poor white] too is saved."[1] After a lifetime of commitment and reflection, Williams despaired that too often the South's literary and academic liberals, and many of its political and social reformers, rejected poor white southerners as a way of distancing themselves from the region's racial practices. Accordingly, they sought to elevate their own standing in the eyes of other liberals, especially northern supporters, by applauding the virtue, cleverness, and courage of blacks while at the same time mocking or ridiculing the social habits of impoverished whites.

A scene from the spring of 1937 graphically portrays the way that this dynamic helped to shape power relationships within the Southern Tenant Farmers' Union (STFU). During National Sharecroppers Week of that year, thousands of New Yorkers attended a meeting at the city's Mecca Temple and watched as three Arkansas sharecroppers, all organizers for the STFU, shared the stage with senators Robert LaFollette and Robert Wagner and Socialist presidential candidate Norman Thomas. According to STFU cofounder and secretary H. L. Mitchell, one of the Arkansas sharecroppers stole the show. Mitchell arrived late at the meeting after LaFollette had already begun speaking, and he was chagrined to realize that "Myrtle [Lawrence] was the center of attraction. She had her 'spit can' covered with bright pink paper, and was busily engaged in using it. The people down front who had the best view of Myrtle's performance were amused, laughing at the sharecropper woman, and paying no attention whatever to the speakers." What was even worse, from Mitchell's perspective, was that Henrietta McGhee, an African American organizer, afterward told him that she was "never so embarrassed in her life as by that old white woman making everyone think the union folks were all just like those Tobacco Road people they had heard about."[2]

When viewed historically, this scene, or Mitchell's account of it, reveals a universe of meaning involving culture, power, race, and gender—themes that are today so compelling to cultural historians of the South. The STFU had been founded in Tyronza, Arkansas, in 1934 as a biracial effort to combat abuses stemming from local enforcement of the New Deal's Agricultural Adjustment Administration (AAA). Under the AAA program, tenants and sharecroppers legally retained their traditional share of the profits from crops they grew, but planters and AAA administrators in the cotton South often ignored this aspect of the national legislation. Owners frequently violated their AAA contracts by demoting tenants and sharecroppers to wage earners or by evicting them from their homes. In 1937 the STFU was at its high tide, claiming a membership of 25,000 in six states. In its first three years of existence, the STFU, along with Dorothea Lange's photographs, introduced the nation to sharecroppers, and it became the chief vehicle through which liberals like theologian Reinhold Niebuhr, civil libertarian Roger Baldwin, and activist Eleanor Roosevelt educated themselves on sharecroppers and rural poverty. In the imagination of many northern liberals, Arkansas as the wellspring of the tenant farmers' movement encoded the cultural and political landscape through which they understood southern sharecroppers and their world. Arkansas meant sharecroppers, and sharecroppers meant the STFU.[3]

Mitchell and other leaders of the STFU were attuned to new intellectual fashions among the country's artists, writers, and scholars as well as a significant portion of the professional classes. By 1933 expatriate writers and artists had come home, helping to underscore the belief that a democracy's cultural and artistic arsenal resides in the lives of ordinary citizens. Whereas in the 1920s the poor had been the subject of artistic disdain, absorbed into "the masses" and not the appropriate subject for creative art, the depression at home and the rise of fascism in Europe had transformed sharecroppers, factory workers, and the unemployed into "the people."[4] As impoverished individuals seeking to better their circumstances by fighting a distasteful oligarchy, STFU sharecroppers became a cherished symbol of America's native strength and democratic commitments.

Mitchell, himself the son of a tenant farmer, was concerned that Myrtle Lawrence, if accepted as a representative sharecropper, would tarnish this STFU icon in the eyes of northern supporters. Well aware that such individuals often found the white southerner's double negatives and tobacco spit as offensive as the region's racial practices, Mitchell guarded the STFU by eyeing Lawrence and his own culture from the perspective of an outsider. By National Sharecroppers Week of 1937, Mitchell had worked tirelessly for three years to establish a solid financial and institutional foundation for the STFU. He had secured legal help for members when they were jailed, and the STFU headquarters in Memphis was overwhelmed with requests for his help. He had, especially in the early years, provided the shaping hand for this fragile institution.[5] As the chief liaison with the outside world, Mitchell negotiated and socialized with powerful men who wrote legislation and books, ran the country's leading newspapers, and preached from its prominent pulpits. Ferociously bright and with a love of books and ideas, Mitchell, however, would continue to be a supplicant for money, support, and encouragement from (mostly) institutionally and financially secure men. Living on

Myrtle Lawrence picks cotton with her son Elvin Lawrence and a friend. Photograph by Louise Boyle. Courtesy of the Kheel Center for Labor-Management Documentation & Archives, Cornell University.

the edge of a world that invited him in but never asked him to stay, he remained a marginalized male.[6]

As such, he was especially vulnerable to outsiders' perceptions of the union members whom he presented to the public. To his chagrin, he realized that evening that snuff-dipping Myrtle Lawrence on the New York stage was not an appropriate subject for Dorothea Lange's photography of haggard southern mothers nor for Norman Thomas's description of "the plight of the sharecropper."[7] Lawrence was, in fact, plainly having a good time in New York sightseeing, meeting celebrities, and representing this romantic biracial southern organization so dear to northern liberal hearts. In his book published forty-two years after the event, Mitchell distanced his own criticism of Lawrence by attributing to Henrietta McGhee attitudes he had directly expressed in draft form.[8] Invoking the voice of an African American woman to characterize Lawrence as disorderly and unpresentable, Mitchell through McGhee criticized Lawrence in terms that "proper" white society often used against black women. In reversing the voice critical of female behavior from white to black, Mitchell described McGhee as finding Myrtle Lawrence, the "old white woman," unworthy of representing a

Myrtle Lawrence relaxes on her front porch. Photograph by Louise Boyle.
Courtesy of the Kheel Center for Labor-Management Documentation & Archives, Cornell University.

biracial organization bent on sustaining its northern liberal base of support. She was "not 'white,' not really,"[9] or, in other words, she was not a "lady." Mitchell thereby stepped into a trap that ensnared more than one southern liberal reformer: pitting clever blacks against "degenerate" whites, he portrayed both without the texture for which Aubrey Williams yearned.

Mitchell relished describing how McGhee had shamelessly exploited northern naïveté. Imprisoned for her union activities and beaten several times, McGhee appeared on the Washington, D.C., social scene later that week detailing her experience with Arkansas planters. Reports of her injuries grew with each retelling until on one occasion Mitchell rushed to assist the bent and hobbling McGhee. She straightened, burst into laughter, and congratulated herself: "Ho, ho, I even fooled Mitch this time."[10] Mitchell concluded that "Henrietta was a natural leader, an actress who could amuse as well as inspire people."[11] Within the STFU after the Mecca Temple meeting, Mitchell promoted McGhee's leadership but curtailed Lawrence's public visibility. Lawrence and McGhee had similar as-

sets: each was amusing, intelligent, and inspiring. Black women, however, could occupy cultural spaces in reform circles forbidden to white women. Women who were "really" white should either be haggard, with what photographers of the 1930s called "*the* look—mournful, plaintive, nakedly near tears," or they should be "ladies."[12]

Myrtle's performance had added significance because the STFU had become a very different organization from the one initially dominated by white male socialists like Mitchell. His displeasure with Myrtle's performance reflected a wide-ranging and growing frustration with the organization that he and other white male socialists had originally shaped. From the beginning, the STFU scrambled categories: a labor union composed of tenant farmers and sharecroppers, a biracial organization in the cotton South, a radical movement with a conservative agenda. The metamorphosis of the organization from one first led by white male socialists to one dominated by the flavor of a southern rural religious revival ignited a flame that burned brightly in the Delta South.

The cotton-planting strike during the spring of 1936 proved pivotal in forging the STFU into a mass movement. The strike was regarded even by the organization as a failure, but the STFU at the grass-roots level emerged that spring with new life oriented around rituals that had appeared in response to violence. By the summer of that year, members had developed a system of signs based on the Masons. Meeting in secret and submitting to a common oath made the STFU dramatically appealing; sharing signs and coded words intensified bonds of connection while also giving practical resources to members who felt vulnerable. All of

STFU members listen to Norman Thomas speak at a union rally outside Parkin, Arkansas, on 12 September 1937. Myrtle Lawrence's oldest son, Olin, is seated on the ground. Photograph by Louise Boyle. Courtesy of the Kheel Center for Labor-Management Documentation & Archives, Cornell University.

this was dismissed as "rigamarole" and hoopla by Mitchell and the Memphis leaders, but they nevertheless conceded that these rituals had solidified the STFU as a grassroots, biracial organization.[13]

When Myrtle Lawrence first heard about the STFU, she thought it was just another new church.[14] Lawrence considered herself a believer and a religious person, but she did not become conventionally pious until later, after she moved to Tampa, Florida, and "met Jesus" in a vision when she was in her fifties.[15] She had been baptized as a Methodist by immersion, although Louise Boyle, who later photographed Lawrence, found it hard to imagine Myrtle going limp for anybody.[16] She was, however, devoted to the Taylor Springs (Alabama) Baptist Church located next to the cemetery where her mother and other Taylor relatives were buried. Furthermore, she always contended that she was a committed STFU

An STFU member nurses her baby while enjoying a joke by the speaker. Photograph by Louise Boyle. Courtesy of the Kheel Center for Labor-Management Documentation & Archives, Cornell University.

member in part because she had taken her union vows from W. L. Blackstone, a Baptist minister whose religious charisma gave him stature in the organization.

In ambiance and practice, by the time Myrtle joined in 1936, the STFU's meetings and organizational life had come to resemble a southern evangelical revival more than a labor organization. Meetings followed the pattern of religious revivals with fiery sermons, passionate exhortations, and emotional hymns. Women in locals, for example, gave testimony about the power of the STFU in Holiness style, witnessing that the Holy Spirit could instantly transform lives through the union.[17] Sixty percent of the organizers were Baptist preachers; ministers interested in the union often brought their entire congregations into the STFU fold.[18] Members transformed their large meetings into something akin to old-fashioned camp revivals where rigamarole, breast milk, and tobacco spit mingled handily with prayer and sermons.[19] Without this reconfiguration, Myrtle Lawrence would never have been drawn to the STFU. Certainly, she would never have been motivated to work on its behalf.

By 1937 the STFU, shaped as it was in the image of the southern evangelical church, provided space in which tenant and sharecropper women and children of both races felt at home. Actually, the STFU was never so much a labor union with tightly controlled rules and procedures as it was a quasi-religious movement through which thousands of people, as families, protested what they perceived as

Women were more literate than men among STFU members. Daughter-in-law Sylvia Lawrence (background, right) and an unidentified woman read the Sharecropper's Voice, *the STFU newspaper, while other members listen to the speaker. Photograph by Louise Boyle. Courtesy of the Kheel Center for Labor-Management Documentation & Archives, Cornell University.*

the government's participation in breaking the covenant between those who owned the land and those who worked it. That rupture directly touched the lives of women like Myrtle Lawrence.

Myrtle Terry Lawrence scrambled categories as readily as did the organization that gave her public visibility; she was a fitting person on whom to project the new shape of the STFU. She was illiterate but articulate, a pace-setting cotton picker but a "lady" in her children's eyes, a racial equalitarian who needed reminding not to call African Americans "niggers."[20] Lawrence and her family, of Colt, Arkansas, joined the STFU during the summer of 1936 during the cotton-picking strike.

Elvin Lawrence chastises sixteen-year-old Sylvia, his new bride (to left of speaker), as his mother and sister (to right of speaker) manifest the same boredom with the exhortations of this fire-and-brimstone preacher at the STFU *rally. Photograph by Louise Boyle. Courtesy of the Kheel Center for Labor-Management Documentation & Archives, Cornell University.*

Early the following year, the Lawrences learned from their landlord, Wynne businessman Raphael Block, that they must leave their home because Block would not provide a "furnish" that spring. Like many Delta women threatened with eviction, Myrtle felt entitled to her home and refused to move. She was convinced that her landlord had declined to extend his arrangement with her family because she and her husband had joined the union. She responded with a promise of increased union activity: "Mr. Block, you've done yourself the worst day's business you ever did when you didn't give me a crop. Because if I'd have had it, I'd have had something to keep me busy part of the time, but now I'll have nothing to do all year but sign up all your tenants in the Union, and I'll do it, too."[21]

Myrtle Terry was born in 1893 into a family whose fortunes had teetered between sharecropping and land ownership. Born in the hilly, hardscrabble country of Lamar County, Alabama, she grew up near Sulligent not far from the Mississippi border. Married at thirteen to Ben Lawrence (also thirteen) and a mother at fourteen, she lived almost her entire life as a sharecropper. The details of her life conform to much that became known about the lives of tenant and sharecropping women during the 1930s.[22]

Myrtle Lawrence tried to prepare fellow members at her local for their first flash-bulb photograph. Surprise and suspicion, however, overcame them. The shades are drawn to conceal their meeting from planters and other opponents of the union. Photograph by Louise Boyle. Courtesy of the Kheel Center for Labor-Management Documentation & Archives, Cornell University.

She attended school for two weeks of the first grade and never returned after that; she began chopping and hoeing cotton when she was six. By 1937 she and her husband had made twenty-eight crops together: twenty in Arkansas, five in Alabama, and three in Mississippi. She missed only one season of cotton work in the period from 1899 to 1937. She was a vigorous worker in the fields, preferring outdoor work to housekeeping. As her daughter-in-law later put it, "She wasn't no housekeeper. Bless her heart."[23] Years later one of her sons would brag that his mother had often been paid an extra wage to set the pace for other workers, including males, in the cotton fields because "she was the best man."[24] Her daughter came more to the point: "Mama wasn't slow at nothing."[25]

Myrtle Lawrence's rise in the STFU was meteoric; she quickly earned a reputation for being an extraordinarily effective organizer. By the spring of 1937 she had come to be regarded as the best organizer of African Americans that the union had. She at times apparently taunted male organizers by volunteering for difficult tasks and dangerous activities that men found too formidable. During the summer of 1937 she went unannounced to the capitol in Little Rock and was granted an audience with Arkansas commissioner of labor E. I. McKinley. She

As Sylvia Lawrence looks on, Myrtle patches a cotton sack and dips snuff on her front porch while holding grandson Ray Kimbrell. Photograph by Louise Boyle. Courtesy of the Kheel Center for Labor-Management Documentation & Archives, Cornell University.

could also call on Governor Carl Bailey, for whom her son had cast three votes in his 1936 gubernatorial campaign, for help if violence were threatened against the STFU. In response to her telephone requests, state troopers were sent at least twice to ensure a safe assembly of STFU members. Her organizational competence was unquestioned and, from all accounts, unsurpassed. Even H. L. Mitchell remembered her as the best white woman organizer the STFU had.[26]

In reflecting on Myrtle Lawrence's career in the STFU, social historian Priscilla Robertson, who lived in the Lawrence home for ten days in 1937, felt that "when Myrtle first got involved in the STFU, she was probably thinking of feeding her family. Then she discovered she had this extraordinary gift."[27] Her charisma no doubt stemmed in part from her intelligence and sense of purpose. But she had additional sources of personal authority that mattered in the Arkansas Delta: she could read fortunes from coffee grounds and discover water with a stick, services she performed without taking pay. Her visionary powers were most dramatically

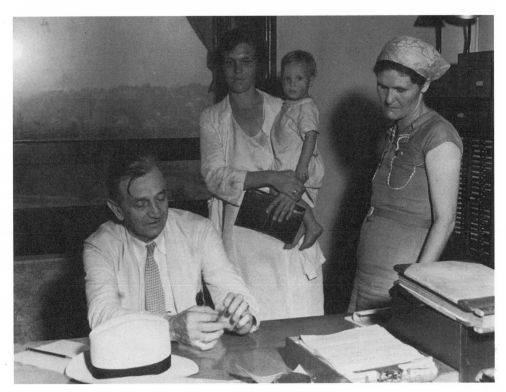

Myrtle Lawrence pays an impromptu visit to the state capitol to call on E. I. McKinley, head of the Arkansas Commission of Labor. Daughter Snow Kimbrell and grandson Ray Kimbrell look on. Photograph by Louise Boyle. Courtesy of the Kheel Center for Labor-Management Documentation & Archives, Cornell University.

witnessed when, for example, she had seen the American flag move across the sky from east to west the night before armistice was declared in November 1918.[28]

When she traveled to New York that spring of 1937, her youngest child was almost twelve; she herself was forty-four. Her rapid rise in the STFU had opened avenues she clearly found exciting and personally gratifying. Myrtle Lawrence met her expanding world with a sense of intrigue and excitement. Most of all, she embraced it with a sense of her own worth. Except for the handicap of illiteracy and embarrassment about pellagra-ravaged teeth, Myrtle manifested a remarkable sense of self-worth. She claimed kinship with Zachary Taylor through her grandmother Nancy Taylor Terry, and she claimed a Native American as her other grandmother. Myrtle Lawrence believed that she owned a piece of the American sky that had so dramatically revealed itself to her in 1918.[29]

In the north Alabama hill country where Myrtle Lawrence grew up, the boundaries separating landowners, tenants, and sharecroppers had been porous. Landowners were often illiterate, and distinctions between the most prosperous and the poor were a matter of degree; being poorer than one's neighbors did not automatically produce an inferiority complex.[30] It was an arena where performing acts of kindness enhanced the status of tenants or sharecroppers, making

H. L. Mitchell
remembered her
as the best white
woman organizer
the STFU *had.*

such individuals respected members of the community.[31] Regional political culture dictated that it was in the best interest of politicians to practice social egalitarianism at least among the white citizenry. The political history of the hill counties of north Alabama tracks a rich tradition of political insurgency expressed in third parties like the Grangers, Agricultural Wheel, Greenback-Labor Party, Knights of Labor, Farmers' Alliance, and the Populist Party. In Myrtle's Lamar County, the Farmers' Alliance had been especially strong.[32] Even today in prosperous areas of northwestern Alabama and northeastern Mississippi, class often refers to a moral universe rather than an economic and educational designation. Factory workers who have labored their entire adult lives at minimum wage can be considered "high class" because of their personal character and community involvement. Avaricious physicians, on the other hand, are "low-class" when they build ostentatious houses and fail to treat poor patients with dignity.[33]

Chinks in the armor of the region's racism could at times be found in the Alabama hill counties. Alabama had not written a miscegenation law until 1852, and interracial couples even then did not face legal charges. Such antebellum unions had often taken place precisely in the northwestern hill counties surrounding Lawrence's Lamar County.[34] Sparsely populated, the area was composed of mostly poor whites and a few blacks. Myrtle Lawrence insisted that her racial beliefs were a part of the way she had been brought up, that she had always been taught that African Americans should be treated the same as whites. Irene Lawrence Witcher confirmed that her mother-in-law's racial views were deep and abiding: "Now, Miz Lawrence just believed that, and she believed it way down deep inside herself. Why, when Bill [Lawrence's youngest son] and I first got married [in 1941] we went to Missouri with Mr. and Miz Lawrence, and we stayed at a black family's home. We slept in their beds and ate at their table. It was just part of her."[35]

When she joined the automobile trip to New York with H. L. Mitchell, Henrietta McGhee, and Dave Griffin, Myrtle could hardly contain her high spirits. In the original draft of his book, Mitchell recalled the drive to New York: "Myrtle Lawrence tried to be the life of the party all the way to New York and was making a play for Griffin who resisted her overtures successfully. We also heard a lot about Myrtle and her family. She had two daughters, both born in the winter. She had named one Icy Jewel and the other Snow[bank]. Myrtle claimed to be the author of a hill billy type song all about 'Down in old St. Francis County, God sent a great big flood. . . .' I can still hear Myrtle's high pitched tuneless voice singing that song."[36]

Mitchell then added, "After the first thousand miles, the rest of us almost wished Myrtle had been drowned in the 'great big flood.' At least no one ever suggested again that Myrtle be sent on a Sharecroppers Week expedition." In a revealing remark, he concluded, "While some tobacco road character[s] got in the Union occasionally, at least 99 percent of both the white and colored members of our Union were honest decent people. Even though they were poverty stricken, joining the Union was evidence of their desire for a better life."[37]

Linking uninhibited social behavior, especially the public emission of bodily fluids, to a moral universe is a practice as old as modernity.[38] By equating Myrtle's tobacco-spitting and (perceived) flirting with dishonesty and indecency, Mitchell revealed a darker side of the liberal imagination toward southern culture and poor whites. Accusing individuals like Myrtle Lawrence of not striving to improve themselves, southern liberals and their northern supporters could with good conscience often write such poor whites out of the covenant of those designated to build a new, more racially inclusive South.[39] Lawrence, of course, would have been surprised to learn that Mitchell regarded her as a Tobacco Road character. Dipping snuff and spitting were part of the cultural landscape in northern Alabama where a proper woman could dip or chew tobacco but not smoke it. Born seven years after Myrtle in a neighboring Mississippi county, Johnnie Morse Hawkins, whose family was regarded as substantial landholders, dipped snuff and recalled that her teachers had cautioned her that "a lady doesn't spit over three feet high on the wall."[40]

Myrtle's children, in fact, regarded her as a lady. When interviewed over forty years after Lawrence had worked with the STFU, Icy Jewel Lawrence Dean emphasized that "she [Lawrence] brought us up to be ladies and gentlemen."[41] Dean's insistence on honoring her mother as a lady underscores that the "lady" was a fluid concept, a construct shaped by local imperatives and claimed by virtually all classes and both races. For Myrtle Lawrence and her family, a lady was a woman who embodied those civic and social virtues favored in the hill area of northern Alabama.

The "lady" as understood in many areas of the hill South was a biblically based notion of womanhood described in Proverbs 31, the scriptural reading often chosen for elderly women's funerals.[42] On such occasions, congregations nodded in communal approval as the minister recited verses 30 and 31: "Favour is deceitful, and beauty is vain, but a woman that feareth the Lord, she shall be praised. Give her of the fruit of her hands; and let her own works praise her in the gates." The Lawrences' conception of a lady was grounded in this notion of womanly virtue.

Jewel Lawrence Dean recounted that "Anything I say you can put in the bank. Mama taught me that. She brought us up to be ladies." Being a lady especially demanded extending hospitality to visitors in the home: "I was raised that when people come, you're supposed to cook them a dinner."[43] Louise Boyle and Priscilla Robertson, who visited in the Lawrence home to document the story of Myr-

Myrtle Lawrence dips snuff on her front porch while holding grandson Ray Kimbrell. "Beats a toothache," Myrtle told Louise Boyle and Priscilla Robertson, regarding her snuff-dipping. Photograph by Louise Boyle. Courtesy of the Kheel Center for Labor-Management Documentation & Archives, Cornell University.

tle Lawrence and the STFU, remembered a scene from their 1937 visit in which Lawrence carefully set a table on her front porch for a black visitor. She prepared the basic fare of greens, peas, and cornbread but added a special dessert of peach cobbler. They commented on the care which attended the preparation of the food and table, even though Lawrence had until recently eaten off lard can tops and drunk from tin cups. Priscilla Robertson recalled of her visit that the Lawrences' "native courtesy was extraordinary, as when Myrtle sent her seven-year-old grandson to press scuppernong grapes into our lips as we lay in bed in the morning."[44]

Dean was convinced that "we come up the best way because we learned how to live and live like you're supposed to and how to make do with what you had and not wish for all that stuff other people's got." When Myrtle Lawrence moved to the Arkansas Delta in 1926, she was offended by the deference patterns and ostentation of the area.[45] She indicted Arkansas planters for their lack of gentility in not bowing to the time-honored reciprocities between owner and tenant. For Myrtle Lawrence, being a lady and a snuff dipper, a labor organizer and a cotton-picker—one who could even pace the men—were compatible. As a southern woman, a sharecropper, and a labor radical, Lawrence had infused the ideal of the lady with meaning that gave her political legitimacy and personal power.

After that spring evening at Mecca Temple, Myrtle Lawrence would no longer appear at fund-raising affairs, and her STFU activities were sharply curtailed. She repeatedly volunteered her organizing services to the STFU headquarters in Memphis, to no avail. The Mecca Temple event was important to Mitchell's justifica-

Snow Kimbrell pours coffee for her family at breakfast. Seated clockwise: John Messemore, daughter-in-law Sylvia's father; granddaughter Lucille Kimbrell; grandson Elroe Kimbrell; son Allen Lawrence; Myrtle Lawrence offering grandson Ray Kimbrell a biscuit; son Elvin Lawrence; Joel Messemore, Sylvia's brother; daughter Icy Jewel Lawrence; daughter-in-law Sylvia Lawrence; and husband Ben Lawrence. Photograph by Louise Boyle. Courtesy of the Kheel Center for Labor-Management Documentation & Archives, Cornell University.

tion of Lawrence's diminished status in the STFU, but her difficulties with the STFU headquarters extended far beyond Mitchell's disapproval. Nearly fifty years later Evelyn Smith Munro, the manager of the STFU's office who had given the organization the only order it ever experienced, recalled with remorse her own response to STFU women like Myrtle Lawrence. A socialist and feminist since her high school years, Smith Munro confessed, "I have to say that she [Lawrence] was just not the kind of woman who interested me at the time. Of course, now I would be completely fascinated by her, but then I was put off by her appearance and mannerisms. And I just do not remember much about the other women like her."[46]

Despite her falling star status in the STFU, Myrtle Lawrence's interest in labor and reform concerns remained high. Several weeks after the Mecca Temple affair,

Myrtle Lawrence and unidentified woman listen to a speaker at an STFU *rally. Photograph by Louise Boyle. Courtesy of the Kheel Center for Labor-Management Documentation & Archives, Cornell University.*

she attended the YWCA's Summer School for Women Workers in Industry in Black Mountain, North Carolina, a school founded to promote self-development in working women. There she learned the rudiments of writing and studied economics under Caroline Ware, a history professor at Vassar College. Lawrence's aspirations matched perfectly the goals of this feminist institution, which was supported by a coalition of northern liberal women and southern middle-class, mostly Methodist, church women.[47] At Black Mountain, the faculty and students regarded her snuff and spitting matter-of-factly, and her professors especially admired her embrace of racial equality, a phenomenon rare among the school's students. As she told the English class at Black Mountain regarding blacks: "They eat the same kind of food that we eat; they live in the same kind of shacks that we live in; they work for the same boss men that we work for; they hoe beside us in the fields; they drink out of the same bucket that we drink out of; ignurance is a kill'n' them just as the same as it's a kill'n' us. Why shouldn't they belong to the same union that we belong to?" [48]

At the summer school, Myrtle was regarded as a model student. Ware and the

Virginia Donaldson Gower poses at Commonwealth College with her portrait of Myrtle and Icy Jewel Lawrence. (Photographer unknown.)

other teachers often asked her to talk with visitors or to give interviews with jour-
nalists from magazines like the *New Masses.* It was on such a visit that she met
Priscilla Robertson and Elizabeth Boyle, journalists originally from Ithaca, New
York. When Boyle mentioned that she had a sister interested in photographing
the South, Myrtle came alive. She had just seen "The Land of Cotton" in the
March of Time, and she had instantly sensed the power of the documentary.[49]

"Myrtle invited Boyle's sister to come to Arkansas, live with us and take all the
pictures she wants," Robertson recalled.[50] In opening her home to Priscilla
Robertson and Louise Boyle, Myrtle set the stage for documenting the story of
the STFU from her perspective. In inviting Boyle to use her life as a human document, Myrtle manifested confidence that her audience would not only find her
struggle interesting but that they would respond with empathy. Entirely missing
from the photographs that Louise Boyle took is "*the* look."

Myrtle remained active at the local level in the STFU for as long as it exhibited
any life in the Arkansas Delta, although H. L. Mitchell remembered her as simply
drifting away, presumably under the influence of Communists in the organiza-

tion.[51] In the fall of 1937 she attended Commonwealth College for several months. In 1939 she bought a small farm as a part of the state's homesteading program, but during World War II, she and her family moved to Tampa, Florida, to work in the city's shipyards. Myrtle would remember her time with the STFU as one of personal achievement, including the acquisition of literacy. However she may have been perceived, she felt constrained only by circumstance. Although the leaders of the STFU essentially banished her from any visible role after her Mecca Temple appearance, Myrtle may have gotten the last word regarding her suitability as a representative of sharecroppers.

In 1976 an oil painting of Myrtle Lawrence and her daughter Icy Jewel, done by Virginia Donaldson Gower in 1937, was selected to appear in "Freedom Expedition," a traveling exhibition that celebrated two hundred years of American history. Hung in a section honoring representative Americans, Lawrence's portrait represented sharecroppers. Thus three women—social historian Priscilla Robertson, photographer Louise Boyle, and artist Virginia Donaldson Gower—aided Myrtle Lawrence in resisting those who would render frozen and one-dimensional portrayals of the South's poor whites. Through the work of these three women, especially the work of Louise Boyle, Lawrence appeals to her compatriots to take a direct look at her—one that transcends patronizing assessments and immediate conclusions.

Myrtle Lawrence's appeal is as compelling as Aubrey Williams's lament was haunting, as historically portentous as it is culturally complicated. Many regarded the STFU as a rehearsal for the Civil Rights movement of the 1960s. Edwin King, chaplain at Tougaloo College in Jackson, Mississippi, during the Civil Rights era, recalled that every person over sixty with whom he worked during that time looked back to the STFU as the spiritual parent of the Civil Rights movement. "They would say, 'Well, we thought that [the STFU] was going to be the time when it would happen, but then we had to wait.'"[52]

With rare exceptions, the faces of poor whites like Myrtle Lawrence were missing from the throngs who joined the biracial protests across the South during the 1950s and 1960s. Their absence raises the question of what the Civil Rights movement might have looked like if southern reformers and their northern supporters had been consistently less concerned with poor white southerners' tobacco spit and double negatives and more focused on local struggles that crossed the boundaries of both race and class.

Myrtle Lawrence's story raises profound questions about the relationship between disadvantaged whites and the course of southern reform. Committed to building a biracial South, Myrtle Lawrence, however, was excluded from the circle of individuals who helped to reshape southern race relations. Labeled "not respectable" and even dishonest for little more than spitting publicly and acting exuberantly, Lawrence was dismissed by the very individuals who represented her organization to the nation's liberals. Historians have yet to write an anatomy of southern liberalism that boldly faces the story of how the region's social activists and academic liberals have often disenfranchised poor whites. In polite conversation in many of the region's academic halls, for example, it is still acceptable to refer to poor whites as "trash," "trailer trash," and "rednecks." If Aubrey Williams was right that the poor of the black South cannot be saved without their white counterparts, then conceptions such as "rednecks" and "trash" must be banished from the discourse of those committed to building a more just society and a more inclusive political culture. Most of all, southerners drawn to a humane vision of the region's possibilities must help to craft a new covenant of reform, one inscribed by all the poor of the South.

NOTES

I thank Elizabeth Jacoway, Mary Frederickson, and Anne Firor Scott for their incisive comments and helpful suggestions when a version of this paper was presented at a panel on "the Southern Lady" at the Fourth Conference of the Southern Association for Women Historians in June 1997. I also thank Kenneth Rutherford, Lynda Coon, Suzanne Maberry, Wayne Flynt, Martha Swain, Suzanne Marrs, Charles Eagles, Ted Ownby, and Charles Reagan Wilson for their comments. I appreciate the assistance of my students David Boling, Fletcher Smith, Laura Lieber, Jennifer Howard, and Elizabeth Propes.

1. Quoted in John A. Salmond, *A Southern Rebel: The Life and Times of Aubrey Willis Williams, 1890–1965* (University of North Carolina Press, 1983), 279–80.

2. H. L. Mitchell, *Mean Things Happening in This Land: The Life and Times of H .L. Mitchell, Co-founder of the Southern Tenant Farmers' Union* (Allanheld, Osmun & Co., 1979), 118.

3. For an institutional history of the Southern Tenant Farmers' Union, see Donald H. Grubbs, *Cry from Cotton: The Southern Tenant Farmers' Union and the New Deal* (The University of North Carolina Press, 1971).

4. See Warren I. Susman, "The Culture of the Thirties," in *Culture as History: The Transformation of American Society in the Twentieth Century* (Pantheon Books, 1973), 150–83.

5. See Mitchell, *Mean Things Happening in This Land*, 27–117.

6. See, for example, Mitchell's self-description as "low man on the totem pole" even at the end of his career as an organizer for the Amalgamated Meat Cutters and Butchers of NA AFL-CIO, Mitchell, *Mean Things Happening in This Land*, 36.

7. Norman Thomas, *The Plight of the Share-Cropper* (League for Industrial Freedom, 1934).

8. Compare draft version of "Henrietta and Myrtle" by H. L. Mitchell, Unprocessed papers of Priscilla Smith Robertson, Vassar College Library, Poughkeepsie, New York (hereafter "Robertson Papers"), with Mitchell, *Mean Things Happening in This Land*, 118.

9. Anthony Walton describes Rick Bragg's family in this manner in "The Hard Road from Dixie" (review of Rick Bragg, *All Over But the Shoutin'*), in *New York Times Book Review*, 14 September 1997, 13.

10. Quoted in Mitchell, *Mean Things Happening in This Land*, 119.

11. *Ibid.*, 119.

12. Quoted in William Stott, *Documentary Expression and Thirties America* (Oxford University Press, 1973), 60.

13. Priscilla Smith Robertson, "A Visit to an Arkansas Sharecropper in 1937," p. II. 3, Undated typescript, Robertson Papers; STFU *Ritual*, ca. February 1938, 7, Southern Tenant Farmers' Union Papers, Wilson Library, University of North Carolina, Chapel Hill; Mitchell, *Mean Things Happening in This Land*, 93–94.

14. Mitchell, *Mean Things Happening in This Land*, 117.

15. Interview with Priscilla Smith Robertson, 19 August 1989.

16. Interview with Louise Boyle, 16 August 1989. It was not uncommon for Methodists to be baptized by immersion in the rural South.

17. Priscilla Robertson remembered a woman in the Pinetree Local entering something like an ecstatic trance after testifying to the power of the STFU. Interview with Priscilla Smith Robertson, 17 August 1989.

18. Jack Temple Kirby, *Rural Worlds Lost: The American South, 1920–1960* (Louisiana State University Press, 1987), 261.

19. See photographs taken at mass rally at Parkin, Arkansas, 12 September 1937, in Louise Boyle Collection, Kheel Center for Labor-Management Documentation & Archives, Martin P. Catherwood Library, School of Industrial and Labor Relations, Cornell University, Ithaca, New York, some of which are reprinted here.

20. Robert B. Duncan, "Notes from Arkansas," *New Masses* (21 December 1937):18.

21. Quoted in Robertson, "A Visit to an Arkansas Sharecropper in 1937," p. I.12.

22. *Ibid.*, 3–4.

23. Interview with Irene Lawrence Witcher, 16 August 1990.

24. Alvin Lawrence to Louise Boyle, 16 October 1982, Tampa, Florida (taped interview in author's possession).

25. Icy Jewel Lawrence Dean to Louise Boyle, 16 October 1982, Tampa, Florida (taped interview in author's possession).

26. Robertson, "A Visit to an Arkansas Sharecropper in 1937," pp. II.1–2; Interview with H. L. Mitchell, 22 February 1989.

27. Interview with Priscilla Smith Robertson, 19 August 1989.

28. Icy Jewel Lawrence Dean to Louise Boyle, 16 October 1982.

29. Robertson, "A Visit to an Arkansas Sharecropper in 1937," p. I.4.

30. Wayne Flynt, *Poor but Proud: Alabama's Poor Whites* (The University of Alabama Press, 1989), 89.

31. *Ibid.*, 209. Homer Flynt, historian Wayne Flynt's grandfather, was an example of this social dynamic.

32. Rose Marie Smith, *Lamar County Alabama, A History to 1900* (Rose Marie Smith, 1987), 180.

33. Interview with Ruth Elizabeth Hawkins Payne, 3 July 1996.

34. See Gary B. Mills, "Miscegenation and the Free Negro in Antebellum 'Anglo' Alabama: A Reexamination of Southern Race Relations," *Journal of American History* 68 (June 1981): 23–25.

35. Interview with Irene Lawrence Witcher, 16 August 1990.

36. Mitchell, Draft, "Henrietta and Myrtle," 2.

37. *Ibid.*, 2–3.

38. See, for example, Norbert Elias, *The Civilizing Process: The History of Manners* (Urizen Books, 1978), 51–160, especially 153–59.

39. See Flynt, *Poor but Proud*, 214–16. For a current expression of this class bias among liberals, note David J. Garrow's attributing the murder of the four children at 16th Street Baptist Church in Birmingham, Alabama, in 1963 to the "murky subculture of truck-stop racists that was at the

heart of the South's worst moments," David J. Garrow, "Back to Birmingham," *Newsweek,* 21 July 1997, 37.

40. Interview with Johnnie Adeline Morse Hawkins, summer 1972.

41. Icy Jewel Lawrence Dean to Louise Boyle, 16 October 1982.

42. As a child in northeast Mississippi, I attended such funerals in the 1950s. I am indebted to Laura Lieber for linking this Hebraic notion of a virtuous woman with the Alabama hill country's concept of the "lady."

43. Icy Jewel Lawrence Dean to Louise Boyle, 16 October 1982.

44. Robertson, "A Visit to an Arkansas Sharecropper in 1937," p. II.17.

45. In 1937, for example, she took Louise Boyle and Priscilla Robertson into Wynne to photograph the Greek revival home of her landlord. At the same time, she listed his shortcomings, including refusing to give her and her husband the lumber with which they could build an outdoor privy. Interview with Priscilla Robertson, 17 August 1989. See Boyle photographs and Robertson, "A Visit to an Arkansas Sharecropper in 1937," p. I.11.

46. Interview with Evelyn Smith Munro, 26 June 1992.

47. For background information on the summer school, see Mary Frederickson, "Recognizing Regional Differences: The Southern Summer School for Women Workers," in *Sisterhood and Solidarity: Workers' Education for Women, 1914–1984,* edited by Joyce L. Kornbluh and Mary Frederickson (Temple University Press, 1984).

48. Quoted in Duncan, "Notes from Arkansas," 18.

49. Robertson, "A Visit to an Arkansas Sharecropper in 1937," p. I.3.

50. Interview with Priscilla Smith Robertson, 19 August 1989.

51. See Mitchell to Robertson, 20 June 1980, Robertson Papers.

52. Interview with Edwin King, 22 February 1997.

Scottish Heritage Southern Style

by Celeste Ray

During the past four decades, growing interest in Americans' cultural and ancestral ties to Scotland has produced hundreds of new clan and heritage societies and a steadily increasing number of Scottish Highland games. Scottish American ethnic awareness and organization has had other, briefer, periods of popularity in our nation's history. However, the growth of Scottish cultural groups and gatherings has proved most dramatic in the late-twentieth-century South, where a unique and distinctly regional style flavors events and perceptions of Scottish origins. Today, approximately half of all Scottish American societies base their associations in the South and more than one-third of the over two hundred annual Highland games/Scottish festivals occur in the region.[1]

The popularity of the Scottish-heritage movement in the South is partly due to its double celebration of a "reclaimed" Scottish ethnicity and its particular relationship to southern regional identity. Southern Scottish-heritage societies emphasize kinship and bill clan society activities as family reunions. Scottish Highland games in the South are more likely to have barbecue stands, fiddle competitions, and time designated for religious events. At southern games, singers perform the Scottish tune "Bonnie Dundee" with the Confederate lyrics "Riding a Raid," reenactors combine Confederate jackets and caps with their Scottish kilts, and bagpipe band renditions of "Dixie" leave crowds either cheering, in tears, or both.

American celebrations of Scottish heritage draw on romantic nineteenth-century interpretations of Highland manners and Scottish identity—a mythic Scottish past that in the South blends harmoniously with nostalgic visions of antebellum southern society and the Lost Cause. Celebratory and commemorative reflections on ancestral experience commonly merge historical realities, religious inheritance, and folk memories with selected (and often invented) traditions to interpret the past in a form meaningful for the present. Southerners take to the Scottish-heritage movement so well because its present form draws on parallel mythologies, rather than actual cultural continuities, that underlie the construction of both Scottish and southern identities. Both derive from perceived historical injuries, strong attachments to place and kin, and links between militarism and religious faith, and both have produced symbolic material cultures.

Scottish-heritage celebration in the South offers alternative interpretations of "southernness." In heritage lore, the southern experience and identity unfold in continuous tradition from Scottish culture and history, rather than from a relationship to slavery or Jim Crow. Members of the southern Scottish American community are of the generations that experienced desegregation and the reinvention of the new South. By attributing southern distinctiveness to Scottish roots, a post–Civil Rights movement celebration of "southernness" takes on an uncontroversial, multicultural dimension focused on ethnic identity rather than race relations. Mourning the Old South's defeat or displaying the Confederate battle flag acquires less problematic meanings in the Scottish-heritage context. The "new southerner" involved in Scottish heritage is no

Carl Ford combines Confederate and Scottish garb at the Biloxi, Mississippi, Scottish Games & Celtic Festival, October 1996. Photograph by author.

longer just a white, Anglo southerner, but an ethnically Celtic southerner with other reasons for being different and unassailable justification for celebrating that difference.

HIGHLANDISM AND THE FORGING OF IDENTITY THROUGH DEFEAT

The Scottish American community celebrates a conception of Scottishness engendered largely by the poet and novelist Sir Walter Scott long after the ancestors of many Scottish Americans had left Scotland. The celebrated heritage is that of one region of Scotland: the Highlands. How the Highlands came to represent the whole of Scotland is quite similar to the way in which plantation owners came to represent southerners generally.

As southern identity focuses on the Lost Cause of Lee and Davis, the Scottish identity of southern Scottish Americans centers on the lost cause of Bonnie

Prince Charlie, whose bid to regain the British throne for the Stuart dynasty ended in 1746 on a Scottish moor called Culloden. Chief among the Jacobites who had supported Charles Edward Stuart against the Hanoverians were the Highland Scots. Although the Highlanders were the most ardent Jacobites, Charlie's defeat resulted in second-class status within Britain for all Scots, and Scotland itself became merely "North Britain" for over a century.

As in the American South, cultural attributes of the vanquished, once no longer a threat, became idealized. Post-Culloden legal proscriptions against Highland cultural expression banned tartan as a symbol of Jacobitism and outlawed bagpipes as "instruments of war." Yet, ironically, the fetishism of Highland culture followed these prohibitions. What the Hanoverian government labeled the dress of traitors, and Lowland Scots had previously associated with cattle thieves, became the Scottish national dress. Lowlanders forsook the ancient Highland/Lowland cultural divide to don tartan and an elaborate and accessorized version of the kilt.

Nineteenth-century Scotland cultivated a particular type of romanticism called Highlandism, or Balmoralism after Queen Victoria's Highland castle. Sir Walter Scott's writings ennobling the hitherto "savage" Highlander, and the subsequent Balmoralism, promoted the well-known militaristic image of the Scot not only as a Highlander but as a bagpiping, kilted soldier. Through the romance of Highlandism, all Scots became defeated Jacobites and Highlanders. It is this image that represents the identity that Americans of Lowland Scots, Scots-Irish, and Highland Scots ancestry alike have "reclaimed" in the heritage movement. It is this identity that articulates well with white southern identity in Scottish-heritage celebration. Created by the battle-driven histories of Scotland and the South, both cultural stereotypes exhibit a certain inventiveness in explaining away defeat by emphasizing the virtues and chivalry of the losers and the romance of lost causes. In southern Scottish-heritage celebration, "Scottish" heritage incorporates the main themes of the Old South Myth—themes originally borrowed *from* Scottish Highlandism.

THE INTEGRATION OF PARALLEL LOST CAUSES

In both the southern and Scottish cases, military defeats become symbolic of the loss of distinctive agrarian ways of life. Folk models position the South's defeat as the end of an aristocratic, privileged, and care-free world for people who valued the extended family and maintained a love of the land and a sense of place. Likewise, the Battle of Culloden marks the demise of Highland Gaelic society and a romanticized, though not prosperous, way of life for a people with clan ties to specific hills and glens. These defeats have become not merely significant in regional histories, but *the* dates after which everything changed for the worse.

Southern antebellum houses, fashions, and manners always stand in opposition to the Reconstruction era. During the forty years following Culloden, legal proscriptions against tartan, bagpipes, and communal clan land ownership accompanied the advent of exorbitant rents and large-scale emigration. Highlanders' sufferings during these years occupy a place in Scottish-heritage literature and event oration comparable to that of Reconstruction in the lore of the South.

In both the plantation legend and Highlandism, the failures of the Confederacy and of Prince Charlie appear to cause major social and economic changes that nonetheless were well underway at the time of the events. Yet the myths portray both the Highland clan system and southern society as functioning smoothly until the dramatic demise of their respective causes at Culloden and Appomattox. The harmonious, pristine, and unchanging nature imputed to plantation and Highland ways of life in commemorative rituals, song, and conversation intensifies indignation at their loss. Southerners comforted themselves in defeat by imagining a noble past, a chivalric pre-war arcadia quite different from northern industrial capitalism. The Highland way of life likewise acquired such romantic associations that even its privations polished nicely into stereotypically Highland sensibility, thriftiness, and efficiency.

In Scottish-heritage lore, Culloden is the reason for broken clan ties and the forced exile of Americans' gallant Jacobite ancestors; in southern lore, the Civil War explains "the fall" of illustrious ancestors and their forced removal from the plantation. Hence, within the southern Scottish American community, "heritage" entails a double sense of loss. Discussion of genealogical research explores what might be now had it just not been for event X in one's southern or Scottish past.

Already familiar with Lost Cause rhetoric and dispossession themes, southerners easily incorporate the experiences of "wronged" Scottish ancestors. It is a central premise in today's heritage lore that the majority of colonial Scottish immigrants fled their homeland as political refugees after Culloden in what is called the Scottish diaspora. Scottish American beliefs that post-Culloden hardships resulted in ancestral immigration inculcate a certain sense of loss and injury—both for the transgenerational loss of a cultural heritage and homeland, and through a revived sense of indignity over ancestral sufferings. John Shelton Reed suggests that white southerners traditionally stand in a certain relationship to the South's Lost Cause and share what he calls a "grievance identity" because of that stance.[2] Such an identity finds a corollary in these particular southerners' "other" heritage of a Scottish identity constructed after Culloden and also grounded in defeat.

Taking on a "Scottish" identity, southerners of Highlander, Lowlander, or Scots-Irish backgrounds stand together on one side of another lost cause, "remember" the wrongs done to the Highlanders, and feel the pique, sometimes passionately, that the injury still smarts. Grievances of southern Scottish Americans include the saga of legal, economic, and cultural repression of Highlanders, the Hanoverian Duke of Cumberland's butchery, and subsequent eviction and forced emigration; southern stories relate parallel grievances of Sherman's March, Republican-implemented "reconstruction," and carpetbaggers. These are often integrated and subtly compared in campfire storytelling and song at Highland games, in heritage publications, at public rituals, and in general discourse about ancestral experience.

A further lament combining southern and Scottish grievances is the tenet that the Civil War deprived the South of its Scottishness. In North Carolina, home to the largest colonial settlement of Highland Scots, the use of the Gaelic language for religious services does seem to have ceased after the Civil War.[3] Following the war, "Scotch fairs" (agricultural fairs) degenerated to occasions for gambling and heavy drinking until their abolition about 1871. Community members suggest that Scottish consciousness succumbed to the overarching implications of the war and the new identity forged by that experience. According to heritage philosophy, coping with the war's devastation meant sublimating Scottish ethnicity, not to an American identity but to a new southern unity. The significance of Culloden faded since most everyone had lost someone in the War of Northern Aggression.

These rationales pardon ancestors for "forgetting to remember." Since heritage lore claims Scottish ancestors did not desert the ancient clan homelands for adventure or profit, but under persecution, they may not be accused of forsaking a heritage that their descendants now value. Those ancestors involved with the Civil War are no less forgiven—their experience being an inheritance itself. Heritage celebration entails reverencing the ancestors; romanticized grievances maintain their venerability in public memory. That a heritage lost was forcibly lost makes its reclaiming particularly potent.

As with Highlandism in Scotland, the plantation legend has become systemic in a southern sense of identity and in the world's conceptions of American southernness. To let go of grievances at this point, in either the Scottish or southern case, would be to let go of the romance as well. Attempts at revising regional identities, even grievance-based identities, are not often popular, especially when such identities have endeared their possessors to the outside world in legend, in public culture, and through tourism.

THE SOUTHERN TAKE ON THE SIR WALTER METHOD

Highlandism developed between 1780 and 1860 with the major thrust of Britain's empire building. Drawing on antebellum origins, southern postbellum lore developed mostly between 1880 and the first quarter of the 1900s. While contemporary southerners recognize the familiar feel and language of Scottish heritage, they credit this to cultural continuity, and, well, heritage. Southern myths are indeed built on a Scottish model, but not of a continuous tradition.

Southern myths assumed a model with which southerners were already well acquainted—the model created through Highlandism and the writings of Sir Walter Scott. Southerners named pets, plantations, and the occasional child after characters and places in Scott's novels. They generally identified with Scott's chivalrous castle- and glen-dwelling characters, who exhibited the best of courtly manners and hospitality, viewing them as models rather than as ancestors. The motifs of Highlandism yielded many parallels for southerners based on assumed spiritual and intellectual kinship rather than "heritage" as is claimed today.

Making aristocrats of patriarchal chieftains, Scott medievalized and feudalized what had been a nonfeudal, pastoralist society in the Scottish Highlands. Southern mythologizing likewise revised a slave society into a courtly realm of knightly lords and beautiful belles. The images and traditions made famous by Scott's Waverley novels provided a favorable analogy to fairly self-sufficient southern plantations in the Cameloting of the Old South. The chivalric moonlight-and-magnolias depiction of antebellum southern society evoked many of the same values and themes as Highlandism.

The lore of the Scottish-heritage movement in the South has been over two centuries in the making. Romantic constructs developed in Highlandizing the Scottish identity proved popular with southerners, who drew from them in idealizing their own Lost Cause. This process produced many apparent similarities between the Scottish Highlands and the antebellum South that Scottish-heritage celebration, and some scholarship, stretches to suggest cultural continuity between the American South and Celtic lands.[4] Southerners are argued to be more Scottish than northern Scottish Americans because of these "authenticating" cultural ties claimed to extend hundreds, even thousands, of years. Certainly Scottish immigrants did contribute to southern culture, but as in the creation of the Old South model, the impact of Sir Walter Scott and Highlandism in current heritage lore cannot be overemphasized.

Scott's influence was much the same in effect in Scotland and in the American South. In Scotland it offered a Highland regional identity that appealed to the Scottish nation. In the South it flavored a postbellum regionalism that appealed to both northerner and southerner. The romanticization of the Highlands and the South was a relief from the tragic consequences of both civil conflicts. It provided a means for reacceptance, as well as remasculinization, of the defeated as representatives of past, but idyllic, ways of life.

The stereotypical image of a Scot as a bagpiping, kilted soldier finds masculine parallels in the characters of southern myth. The Highland soldier is not unlike the military model of the southern gallant: a gentleman and a colonel. Highlanders and southern men have somehow become both heroic in defeat *and* famed for loyal military service to their former enemies following those defeats. Both the South and the Scottish Highlands have disproportionately contributed to their national militaries since their respective disasters. While the Spanish-American War allowed southerners to reaffirm their American patriotism, Scottish Highlanders often took "the king's schilling" rather than face emigration, and their role in British empire-building aided their conversion through Highlandism from traitors to loyal "King's men." "Having been enshrined in their lost cause," writes Nina Silber, "southern men seemed to be permanently cast in a military mold."[5] Likewise, the Highlander, once defeated, is perpetually dressed for battle with claymore in hand. These male icons, prominent in both southern and Scottish mythologies stemming from defeat, are isomorphic in southern Scottish-heritage celebration.

Military professionals comprise a significant portion of the Scottish-heritage community in the South. They merge pride in career and American patriotism with pride in "family" heritage by combining military shirts, badges, and medals with a kilt of their clan tartan. They may also choose from tartans designed for each branch of the U.S. military or opt for a general "U.S. Forces Tartan." Occasionally, event attire incorporates Confederate colors or even portions of Confederate uniforms.

Military members of the southern Scottish community tend to be not just the rank and file, but members of the Army's Special Forces, the Navy Seals, and officers from various branches. By invitation, war veterans may join the national Scottish-American Military Society founded in 1980 in North Carolina and headquartered in Charlotte. Members often credit their career paths and success to their Scottish and southern ancestry, which in heritage lore entails genetic and cultural tendencies to the "martial spirit." Heritage celebration compares and combines the legacies of these "war-like" but "noble and righteous" ancestors.

Romanticization praises, yet tempers, southern and Highland bellicosity by directing it to the service of lost causes. Southern slave owners have transformed into gallant, chivalrous gentlemen, and Highlanders, once known to the outside world only as feuding bandits, are now "Prince Charlie's own loyal and gallant men," possessors of exemplary, noble virtues. The male ideal of southern Scottish heritage has developed as an alloy of the southern cavalier and the Highland warrior.

The southern cavalier is important in southern visions of Scottish heritage as

left: *A product of Highlandism: a gentled warrior of Clan MacLachlan by Robert McIan in 1845.*
From R. R. McIan and James Logan, The Clans of the Scottish Highlands: Costumes of
the Clans *(1845; Alfred Knopf, 1980).*
right: *David Dysart of Kentucky displays a spiked targe and McIanesque attention to detail, July 1995.*
Photograph by author.

a descendant, literally and spiritually, of the Highland clansmen. Scottish heritage
enthusiasts celebrate this link as newly discovered, yet it actually appears in an
earlier period of southern myth-making. Heritage lore posits the eclipse of Scottish identity in the South by the Civil War, yet D. W. Griffith's 1915 *Birth of a Nation* demonstrates the survival of its less palatable associations. Eulogizing the
Old South and describing the origins of the Ku Klux Klan (KKK), Griffith originally titled his film *The Clansman* after its inspiration, a 1905 novel by the Reverend Thomas Dixon. The film links the KKK's use of a flaming cross to a similar
device used by Highland chiefs for summoning clansmen to battle.

Griffith's derivation argument is not well known within the Scottish American
community; it is only the older members who indicate concern about the recent
popularization of a public ritual incorporating the fiery cross at southern Highland games. In a ritual gathering of the clans on the evening before the games,
representatives of each participating clan society symbolically answer the "summons" to their heritage. Positioned on the games field in the shape of a St. Andrew's Cross, they carry flaming torches to be tossed onto a central bonfire as
they announce their clan's presence at the games. Participants seem unaware of
the implications such an event might have had in Griffith's day. In fact, heritage

Retired and active military men "pull a coin check" at the Grandfather Mountain Games in North Carolina, July 1995. Coins received on achieving a certain military status are to be carried at all times; in the eventuality that one person does not have the coin, all present are owed a drink. Photograph by author.

lore leaves a gap in southern-Scottish awareness between the Civil War and the "revival" of the latter twentieth century. However, today's Scottish heritage participants do explicitly distinguish clan from "klan" and link southerner and Highlander predominantly through ideal male virtues.

ICONOGRAPHY: TARTAN AND THE CONFEDERATE FLAG

Material expressions of identity, lost causes, and the whole mythologies of Highlandism and the Old South meld in the combination of tartan and the Confederate flag. As markers of cultural identity, these icons visually reference the Highland and Old South legends, the concept of clan as family, and regional heritage. Both have come to symbolize "eras" that met with dramatic ends and "forgotten" parts of the American experience. Tartan and flag combine at Scottish-heritage events in the reclaiming of identities once suppressed "for the greater good." As descendants of Scottish settlers replaced Scottish with southern identities, their descendants supplanted both identities with a reaffirmed sense of American patriotism during the world wars. Post–World War II heritage revivals developed in the new high of American superpower status and evidence the resurgence of regionalism following the unifying experience of that war. Today, those claiming a Scottish identity or displaying a Confederate flag do not consider themselves unpatriotic. Rather, the identities represented by the flag and the tartan embody those values that participants now feel make them "better" Americans.

Commonly called plaid by most Americans, tartan is a badge of membership within the Scottish community, and one's choice of tartan signifies both clan affiliation and knowledge of clan and Scottish history. The link between clan name and tartan pattern, or sett, is largely a nineteenth-century innovation. Originally an effective merchandising strategy in the Balmoralism craze and in tourism, the association between clan name and sett has nonetheless *become* traditional. Tartan

A color guard from the Scottish-American Military Society leads a "Tartan Parade" as the pipe-band following plays "Dixie." First annual Culloden, Georgia, Highland Games, 1995. Photograph by author.

is omnipresent at heritage events, and in this context, it symbolically evokes the whole history and mythology of the eighteenth-century Highlanders' experience, the loss of this heritage, and its reclaiming.

Each clan tartan has come to represent a unique clan story, and telling and debating these stories is part of wearing the tartan. After discovering their clan tartan, many participants first learn about things-Scottish through the history of the clan with which they share a surname and, by enthusiastic extension, "a kinship." Southern Scottish-heritage events evidence a greater emphasis on clan and kinship than do those in the North or West. The Scottish American community is organized into general heritage societies and specific clan societies. Membership in the latter allows one to "rediscover" one's "cousins." Participants join clan societies that bear their surname or that of an ancestor. Members often assume that even those sharing names derived from occupations such as "Smith" or "Forrester" are necessarily kin. Actually, the large numbers of MacDonalds or Mac-Neils stem not from remarkable ancestral fecundity, but from the progenitors of today's MacDonalds or MacNeils allying themselves with a clan chief of that name at a time when most people did not need last names. Though the clan system was historically Highland, those with surnames of Lowland origin now form

Clan MacFie parades their "Clan Commander" as an honored Highland games guest, October 1995. Pendants attached to the clan's tartan banner note the battles in which the MacFies have participated. Some southern clan branches also commemorate Civil War battles fought by southern bearers of the clan name. Photograph by author.

clan societies—something which, along with the wearing of tartan, would dismay their revered ancestors.

At southern Highland games, clan tents overshadow the actual athletic competitions. These tents display artifacts, books, and interpretation related to clan history. They also serve to recruit new members. First-time visitors to the games locate relevant tents to learn about their "family" history, and clan society members stop by their tents to visit with their "cousins" and chat about genealogy. At large southern games such as those held at Stone Mountain near Atlanta or the South's premier games at Grandfather Mountain in Linville, North Carolina, well over one hundred clans represent themselves on the games fields. Even at small southern games, clan tents are the central focus. In contrast, northern games may field fewer than a dozen clan tents, and in Scotland, clan tents are not a part of Highland games. The southern emphasis on "blood kinship" within the clan is a further elaboration of Highlandism: not only does each clan have a specific tartan, but all who wear the tartan are "kin."

Pedigree-conscious southerners may obtain one through Scottish heritage. Simply by having a Scottish last name one acquires new "kin" through clan membership, an ancient and illustrious past, and a new sense of place in a "homeland" one may never visit—the historic landscapes of the clan lands. As southern mythologizing supplies an elite, planter background and great house for those whose ancestral greatness is no longer apparent "because of the War," Scottish heritage lore enhances the "backgrounds" of those planters with chieftains in the "family" tree and castles in the "family" lands.

Associating clan with kin means that tartan operates as a type of heraldry. By donning a tartan one claims the heroic deeds of clansfolk as one's own heritage and the aristocrats of the clan as one's own "cousins." Within the community, tartan immediately distinguishes one not only as a Scottish American but as a Buchannan, Campbell, or Cameron. The wearer of tartan becomes a bearer of the clan reputation. Consciousness of clan history leads to awareness of "traditional" clan enemies—also identifiable by the tartans they sport. As clan feuds are researched and discussed by participants, they are born again, in a more playful way, on the Scottish Highland games field.

The large-scale Scottish-heritage movement in the American South is such a relatively new thing that being the first of one's family to rediscover the family Scottish heritage elicits congratulations rather than condescension as might be expected. Newly reborn Scots tend to place a special emphasis on the long loss of tradition and on ancestral grievances. Those claiming Scottish origins after discovering a Scottish surname in their genealogies also tend to display tartan with more enthusiasm than those with a transgenerational awareness of their Scottish ancestry. Southerners come to their Scottish roots in different ways, but what they share is a lifetime awareness of their southern identity—a kind of primary ethnic identity upon which the Scottish identity layers.

The familiar Confederate battle flag is also present at Highland games and heritage events on T-shirts or lapel pins, on bumper stickers, and side-by-side with American and Scottish flags in clan society tents and in Highland games campgrounds. Believing their southern heritage to be an extension of their Scottish heritage, members of the southern-oriented Heritage Preservation Association describe their flag-bearing association T-shirts as appropriate attire for Scottish events. They emphasize the flag's incorporation of the Scottish flag's St. Andrew's Cross, which is also a symbol, for many, of the Confederate states.

Both tartan and the Confederate flag encode beliefs about ancestry, but a difference in their symbolic power is obvious. Though proscribed for nearly forty years, tartan regained acceptance through the British army's efforts to recruit Highlanders. In that context, tartan was transformed from the garb of rebels to that of valorous Highland soldiers loyal to the Crown. The meaning of the Confederate flag, in contrast, is still a source of contention. Those who fly the flag at Scottish events speak of the South in romanticized terms: of the cult of chivalry and southern belles, "aristocratic" southern manners, and Bonnie Robert E. For them the Confederate flag symbolizes something quite different from what its detractors perceive; it symbolizes the Old South as the product of their idealized Scottish ancestors' further idealized accomplishments and the loss of both Scottish and southern traditions. Likewise, tartan, gussied up in the nineteenth centu-

Doug Ross exhibits his collection of Ross Rifles, originally designed by a member of his clan. Loch Norman Highland Games, Charlotte, North Carolina, 1996. Photograph by author.

ry, symbolizes the vision of Highland life from the Victorian period. Although those Highland Scots who came to the South adjusted their attire for the climate, the Scottish American adoption of Highland dress and distinctive tartan setts provides an iconography to a generalized—and more easily assumable—heritage. Southern states initiated the development of state tartans, the first being North Carolina, Georgia, and Texas. In 1997 the interweaving of Scottish and southern heritage found both literal and symbolic expression with the Alabama introduction of a Confederate Memorial Tartan featuring a sett of Confederate gray and battle-flag red. In this way, through costume and imagery, simplified visions of both "Highlandness" and "southernness" are comparable and blended by those raised on the latter. Southernness becomes an unproblematic outgrowth of ancestral proclivities.

HERITAGE AND THE "FAITH OF THE FATHERS"

Charles Reagan Wilson has called the ritual commemoration of the Lost Cause a civil religion.[6] Southern Scottish heritage celebration might well be similarly labeled. The remembrance of both southern and Jacobite lost causes employs religious metaphors in commemoration of secular events and artifacts that have acquired a sacred sense as heritage.

Wilson notes that Civil War artifacts have a "sacred aura"; similarly, those of the Jacobite period (locks of Bonnie Prince Charlie's hair, sheets on which he had slept, crystal glasses or jewelry with his image) are venerated as "relics" today. Contemporary images of Charlie and Flora MacDonald, the woman who helped him escape Hanoverian clutches, abound not only in Scottish representations of national identity (from touristic advertising to shortbread packaging), but also in heritage paraphernalia (in pictorial images "for the home," on desk sets and stationery, on CD jackets of "traditional" tunes, on tableware, and, of course, T-shirts). Like tartan and the Confederate flag, these images instantly invoke the whole of their respective heritage lores.

The reverence and devotion accorded such symbols find more explicit expression in actual worship services focused on the heritage of faith. Scottish heritage events in the South often have religious, especially Presbyterian, portions that affirm the importance of faith in a secular age and link faithfulness to ancestral virtues. Such events show the influence of southern Protestantism in the use of evangelical language and references to "finding" or "coming to" the heritage. Celebrants often speak of this discovery as a conversion experience. Community members claim "converts" and like to be acknowledged for "shepherding" new members into "the Scottish fold." Just as responding to God's will is answering, heeding, or hearing "the call," so too does one "hear the call" to one's own heritage.

Heritage language also mixes military with religious metaphors. The emphases on Presbyterianism and military prowess combine in the virtuous service of noble causes. The southern knight is a Christian soldier, and the Scottish Highlander of heritage lore becomes both the ideal warrior *and* Presbyterian. Actually, Highlanders originally opposed Presbyterianism by fighting on the Crown's behalf against the Lowlander Covenanters. The history behind the heritage metamorphoses, however, in the southern construction of Scottish ethnicity.

Southern Scottish-heritage events celebrate Covenanter-style Presbyterianism with new rituals of Highlandism. Outlawed in the seventeenth century, Covenanters' religious meetings, called "conventicles," took place illicitly, out-of-doors and surrounded by armed guards. Today, a worship service honoring Scottish ancestors, called a Kirkin' O' the Tartan, often takes place in an open field to emulate conventicles. Interestingly, the "guards" for these services are reenactors in the stereotyped tartan dress of Highland soldiers, who actually attacked Covenanters, and the Kirkin' concludes with a blessing of the tartan—the fabric Lowland Covenanters associated with enmity. A further convolution involves the stressed link between religious faith and faithful labors for lost causes. Fidelity to Prince Charlie made heroes of the Highlanders, but Prince Charlie was loyal to Catholicism, an attachment that had denied his father the crown.

When history becomes heritage, Highland/Lowland and religious divisions

NATCHEZ
Fall Pilgrimage

October 3-26, 1997
Natchez, Mississippi

The annual Natchez Fall Pilgrimage promotional brochure features models in tartan hoopskirt and child's Scottish Glengarry near an ancient southern oak and columned plantation house. Courtesy of Natchez Pilgrimage Tours.

vanish in the face of the more emotive Culloden. As nineteenth-century southerners perceived themselves loyal to their faith despite the moral issues involved in their lost cause, their descendants likewise hold religion very dear and very flexible. Celebrations of the past often blend exactly what forebears found most divisive. In southern Scottish-heritage celebration, participants fuse portions of the past into a unified heritage built on collective, rather than specific, grievances; on a particular faith, rather than historic diversity; and upon warrior ethics that also suit "gentlemen."

REVITALIZATION AND THE SOUTHERN VIEW OF SCOTTISH HERITAGE

Just as their creation originally served social needs, the revival and elaboration of both Highlandism and the southern myths in conjunction show that the new South is not so done with the old. The movement to revive a "heritage lost" and efforts to maintain the grievance identities themselves reveal a basic dissatisfaction with the order of things. The Scottish-heritage movement, as expressed in the American South, corresponds with what anthropologists call a revitalization movement: an intentional and organized attempt to create a more satisfying state of existence.

In their conscious attempts to recreate community and retrieve a sense of identity or ethnicity that participants feel to be lost, heritage celebrations may be considered a response to post-modernity. But here Anthony Wallace's distinction between a revitalization movement and revivalism proves relevant. He defines the aim of the latter to be the "return to a former era of happiness, to restore a golden age, to revive a previous condition of social virtue."[7] Celebrating the past and wanting to be in the past are vastly different phenomena. Scottish-heritage celebration calls for a return only to ancestral "values" and the security that predecessors are presumed to have had in their identity—the type of security born in moments of societal drama. Today's drama comes from within and plays out in culture change rather than lost causes. Southern Scottish-heritage enthusiasts do not claim the South or the Jacobites will rise again, but they do commemorate what they perceive to be southern and Scottish virtues as instructive for the present and as secure moorings at a point in history in which change seems more rapid.

By definition, mythologizing processes construct contrasts to the present. As a revitalization movement, the celebration of Scottish heritage in the South reflects what participants feel is happening to their own society, especially with regard to kin ties, faith, and gender identities. According to heritage tradition, Culloden dispersed the clans; delocalization of the American labor force, which southerners resisted for so long, distances families from each other and from southerners' peculiar attachment to place. Heritage pilgrims join clan ("family") societies and visit places made sacred by their historic ancestral associations— both in the South and in the ultimate pilgrimage to the Scottish clan lands.

The shape of heritage lore also echoes recent, dramatic changes in American gender roles. A central grievance of clan societies is the legendary demise of the clan chief's paternal role and unquestioned authority following Culloden. The heritage movement's emphasis on southern and Scottish military traditions and on patriarchically structured clan societies portrays such masculine roles as both ancient and proper. Within the context of Scottish heritage, male identities are secure and their celebration is the most expressive. It is

"Chief Chinubbie," son of the chief of both Clan Macintosh and the Creek, greets visitors to the clan tent at the Stone Mountain Highland Games, Georgia, 1995. Photograph by author.

the men who wear tartan costumes and who are on display. Women, for whom true kilts are off-limits, have fewer options for exhibiting tartan in the Scottish style. However, southern women are blending traditions to develop new strategies for heritage dress. In Georgia, Alabama, and Mississippi, hostesses of antebellum home tours are increasingly incorporating their clan tartans in the costume of the hoopskirted belle.

Stirred by the wake of Alex Haley's *Roots* and the post–Civil Rights movement emphasis on diversity, contemporary interests in ethnicity and in genealogical hobbies figure significantly in celebrations of all alternative American identities. Scottish and southern identities do not mingle alone at southern Scottish heritage events. John Reed notes that "southerners are more likely to claim Indian ancestry than are nonsoutherners,"[8] and Scottish-heritage events in the South are

Heritage commodified: T-shirts for sale at the 1996 Gulfport, Mississippi, Highland Games set "Moonlight and Magnolias" alongside a sword-waving Scottish "Lion Rampant." Photograph by author.

more likely to reference Native American heritage and ancestry than similar events in the North. Southern Scottish Americans might send their children to both Highland dancing competitions at Scottish games and Native American dancing competitions at southern Pow Wows. Native American trading, social, and kin links with Scots find recognition in dress, reenactment, and story at southern Scottish gatherings. Scottish heritage is absorbed into the southern identity on the Old South model, but in the 1990s, even old mythologies can be further romanticized in a multicultural form.

Focusing on the Highlandism and romanticization that underpin the southern Scottish-heritage movement serves not to explode myths or deconstruct invented traditions, but rather to emphasize how perceptions of the past influence not only celebration but also conceptions of identity and the present. Far from being escapist, romanticization of past failures and hardships secures a sense of self in times of change. The celebrated past, refined and polished, sets precedents for today in the guise of "heritage."

In the southern celebration of Scottish heritage we see the synthesis of two similar romantic traditions. Highlandism transformed the impoverished Scottish Highlands from a land of treacherous insurgents into one of the last bastions of true chivalry, gracious hospitality, and religious fortitude—something of the ideal that southerners claimed as their own after the Sir Walter model. The celebration of Scottish heritage in the South may overlook the Scottish Highland/Lowland cultural divide, but the division between the American North and South still plays a powerful role in the claiming of identity.

NOTES

1. Figures are based on Games listings annually compiled by Jim Finegan of the Clan MacLachlan Association of North America. I include the following twelve states under the rubric

of "southern": Alabama, Arkansas, Florida, Georgia, Kentucky, Louisiana, Mississippi, North Carolina, South Carolina, Tennessee, Texas, and Virginia.

2. John Shelton Reed, *The Social Psychology of Sectionalism* (University of North Carolina Press, 1983), 83.

3. James MacDonald, "Cultural Retention and Adaptation Among Highland Scots" (Ph.D. dissertation, University of Edinburgh, 1993), University of Edinburgh Library.

4. See Grady McWhiney, *Cracker Culture: Celtic Ways in the Old South* (University of Alabama Press, 1988); Grady McWhiney and Perry D. Jamieson, *Attack and Die: Civil War Military Tactics and the Southern Heritage* (University of Alabama Press, 1982); James Michael Hill, *Celtic Warfare* (John Donald Publishers, 1986).

5. Nina Silber, *The Romance of Reunion: Northerners and the South 1865–1900* (University of North Carolina Press, 1993), 173.

6. Charles Reagan Wilson, *Baptized in Blood: The Religion of the Lost Cause* (University of Georgia Press, 1980), 170.

7. Anthony Wallace, "Nativism and Revivalism," in *Magic, Witchcraft and Religion*, ed. Arthur Clehmann (Mayfield, 1985), 319–24.

8. John Shelton Reed, "The Cherokee Princess in the Family Tree," *Southern Cultures* 3 (Spring 1997): 111–13.

Race, Sex, and Reputation
Thomas Jefferson and the Sally Hemings Story

by Robert M. S. McDonald

*B*y August 1802, the image of Thomas Jefferson had not yet been carved in stone, but it had at least been molded in wax. The likeness of the third president stood alongside twenty-four other famous figures on display in Georgetown. Adults handed over fifty cents to view the traveling exhibit; children paid half-price. Had this mobile wax museum been situated to the south, in Richmond, the paraffin statues might have toppled. An earthquake rocked the Virginia capital; its noise, according to one published report, resembled "the roaring of a chimney on fire."

Less than a month later, the *Richmond Recorder* created shock waves of its own. Threatening a similar potential to damage the president's image, these rumblings came in the form of charges levied by the newspaper against Jefferson's character. Around the environs of Monticello, the journal asserted, "it is well known that the man, *whom it delighteth the people to honor*, keeps, and for many years past has kept, as his concubine, one of his own slaves. Her name is SALLY." In the 1780s, Sally had lived in her master's Parisian household during his diplomatic mission to France and gave birth to their first child, according to the account, within nine months of their return to America. "The name of her eldest son is TOM. His features are said to bear a striking, although sable resemblance to those of the President himself." Jefferson's "wench" had borne him "several children"—a later report set the number at five—and "not an individual in the neighborhood of Charlottesville" did not "believe the story."[1]

Written by James Thomson Callender, a Scottish émigré and one-time Republican whom Jefferson had recently passed over for a federal job, the accusation reverberated through the Federalist press. "We have heard the same subject spoken of in Virginia, and by Virginia gentlemen," claimed the *Gazette of the United States*. The *Connecticut Courant* held that Callender's "convincing" charges "startle the most impudent" and confirm that Jefferson "is in every respect unfit to be the head of any people not lost to decency or given over to reprobation."[2]

On the issue of his purported sexual conduct, as on other personal matters brought forth by detractors, Jefferson remained silent before the public. More

46

than a decade later, Jefferson wrote that the best and—for him—only answers "to federal slanders" could be produced through "the tenor of my life, half a century of which has been on a theatre at which the public have been spectators, and competent judges of it's [*sic*] merit." The widespread confidence in his character by then confirmed "that the man who fears no truths has nothing to fear from lies."[3]

Historians have labored for decades to cast doubt on Callender's assertion that the president engaged in a long-term affair with Sally Hemings. The evidence, however, remains inconclusive, and the paternity question—unresolved and, short of DNA tests, probably unresolvable—is getting more attention than ever.[4] But the ongoing speculation about Jefferson's guilt or innocence ignores a more historical, if less sensational, aspect of the Sally Hemings saga: namely, the light that Callender's accusation and Americans' subsequent reactions shed on the dynamics of public opinion in the early republic. Like the Richmond earthquake, rumblings generated by rumors of a Jefferson-Hemings affair neither lasted long nor caused much damage. By the end of 1802, after citizens bestowed upon their president an overwhelming vote of confidence during midterm congressional elections by bolstering Republican majorities in both the House and the Senate, the Federalist outpouring of attacks on Jefferson's supposed amour had slowed to a

The Richmond Recorder,
2 September 1802, in which Callender
first published the allegations.
Courtesy of the Library of Virginia.

trickle. Little was said about Hemings, for example, in the months before his 1804 landslide reelection, and only infrequently during the remainder of Jefferson's lifetime did references to the alleged affair appear in print.[5]

Callender made clumsy use of race and sex as political issues. He indicted Jefferson for undermining the hegemony of white Americans, but he also overestimated his own credibility and misunderstood anxieties over miscegenation. In addition, he failed to perceive that some of his contemporaries would resist confusing accusations of personal misdeeds as verified acts of public wrongdoing. As a result, the story that he hoped would serve as a funeral dirge for the

Short of
DNA tests,
the paternity
question is
probably
unresolvable.

president's political career merely produced a sour note. Even after widespread circulation of the allegations relating to Sally Hemings, Jefferson's image remained largely unscathed.

FEAR OF MISCEGENATION
AND OTHER RACIAL ANXIETIES

As introduced by Callender and as proffered by many Federalist prints, the Jefferson-Hemings story exploited racial anxieties, particularly fears of miscegenation. If the tale were true, the president would be a fornicator, dabbling out of wedlock in the pleasures of the flesh. Moreover, this extramarital affair might have marred the morals of his children, grandchildren, and other relatives, many of whom resided on Jefferson's mountaintop within earshot of his purportedly tempestuous bed. Finally, he would be guilty of bastardy. The Callender charges, however, did not address these crimes. Instead, Jefferson stood accused of lusting after and loving a black woman. Worse than simple bastards, this romance produced mulattoes.

Lest anyone forget the heritage of the president's supposed mistress, press pieces variously referred to her as an "African Venus" and a "black Venus," as "Dusky Sally," "Black Sal," "Sooty Sal," "a sooty daughter of Africa," "the copper coloured Sally," and the "mahogany colored charmer" who headed Jefferson's "Congo harem." In the *Boston Gazette* appeared a mock madrigal from Jefferson to his slave. Here, as elsewhere, pigment preoccupied the author's attention:

> In glaring red, and chalky white,
> Let others beauty see;
> Me no such tawdry tints delight—
> No! *black's* the hue for me!
> Thick pouting lips! how sweet their grace!
> When passion fires to kiss them!
> Wide spreading over half the face,
> Impossible to miss them.
> Oh! Sally! hearken to my vows!
> Yield up thy sooty charms—
> My best belov'd! my more than spouse,
> Oh! take me to thy arms!

Similarly, articles reminded readers that the interracial union produced "a yellow son," nearly half a dozen "mulatto children," and that Jefferson chose "an African stock where upon he was to graft his own descendants."[6]

The notoriously lascivious behavior of American slaveholders lent credence to Callender's charges. John Adams in 1810 repeated the claim of one southern woman that not a single Virginia planter "could not reckon among his slaves a number of his own children." Noting that southern family trees oftentimes possessed both aristocratic and slave branches, Kentucky emancipationist David Rice said in 1792 that "men will humble their own sisters, or even their aunts, to gratify their lust." As a result, "Fathers . . . have their own children for slaves, and leave them as an inheritance to their own [white] children." It was a "mathematical certainty," he held, "that if things go on in the present channel, the future inhabitants of America will inevitably be Mulattoes."[7] At Monticello, twisted lineages reinforced Rice's remarks.

Regardless of Jefferson's own guilt or innocence of miscegenation, race-mixing tainted his plantation family. Hemings and her enslaved siblings were noticeably light-skinned, and quite possibly they shared the same father as Jefferson's wife, who had died in 1782. If so, the president's inheritance from John Wayles, his father-in-law, included not only considerable wealth in land and slaves, but also his wife's half-brothers and half-sisters. No wonder he contended that miscegenation "has been observed by every one."

Through his writings, Jefferson stood as a leading and lifelong opponent of the intermingling of black and white blood. He recoiled at the notion of miscegenation in his *Notes on the State of Virginia*, written only a few years before his alleged love affair supposedly began. Suspicious that blacks were "inferior" to whites "in the endowments both of body and mind," he maintained that slaves, when emancipated, should be "removed beyond the reach of mixture" and colonized beyond the borders of the United States. His opinion did not change. In 1826, just months before his death, he informed his friend William Short that America's slaves should be freed and then expatriated to the West Indies. This, he told Short, would prevent miscegenation, to which he had always possessed "great aversion." Others shared his distaste for race-mixing. Massachusetts governor and Jefferson ally James Sullivan, for example, proposed education and gradual emancipation for America's enslaved blacks but could not help worrying "that it will tend to a mixture of blood, which I now abhor." Fears of miscegenation were much less acute in New England, however, which had only a fraction of the number of blacks the South did. As Jonathan Edwards observed, "Negroes in these northern states also will, in time, mix with the common mass of the people. But we have this consolation, that they are so small a portion of the inhabitants, when mixed with the rest, they will not produce any very sensible diversity of colour."[8]

Not surprisingly, in the North, where miscegenation posed little threat, Jefferson's enemies capitalized on the scandal as an opportunity for mirth. Massachusetts Congressman Thomas Dwight, for example, struck a sardonic tone after attending an 1803 reception at the Executive Mansion. "If black Sal was in the

The "Philosophic Cock," cartoon. Courtesy of the American Antiquarian Society.

house," he told his wife, "she certainly did not appear in the drawing room or audience hall." Federalists must have crowed over a cartoon, titled "A Philosophic Cock," depicting Jefferson and Hemings as lovebirds. Glib newspaper essays similarly portrayed the president as a lusty scientist, examining Sally in an attempt to more fully discern the amorous capabilities of her race. After first mentioning the supposed Hemings romance and then describing Jefferson's low opinion of African Americans and of the mixing of black and white blood, Maryland's *Frederick-Town Herald* announced that "much matter of entertainment may now be connected." Perhaps, the paper speculated, the Sally Hemings affair "has been merely a course of practical experiments, by the result of which Mr. Jefferson was afterwards moved to alter his first opinions." Callender's accusation gave northern Federalists not only merriment but also another angle from which to portray the president as a hypocrite on issues of race. Even before his charges saw print, at least one editor had wondered aloud whether a statesman who relied for sustenance on "half-naked, ill-cared for slaves" could truly be "a mighty democrat—a warm stickler for the *rights* of man."[9]

Northerners may have joked about the rumors, but in the South miscegenation was seen as no laughing matter. Tense race relations rocked the Chesapeake in the first years of the nineteenth century, as slave rebellions caused citizens to fear for their lives. Only months before the Callender story surfaced in print, five slaves swung from the gallows at Halifax, Virginia, sentenced to die for conspiring to revolt. In the nearby North Carolina town of Windsor, a similar scene took place a month later. Many whites reeled in horror at the prospect of a looming black revolution. It may be no coincidence that Callender, racist to the core and easily persuaded by conspiracy theories, chose to circulate rumors of Jefferson's reputed interracial relationship in September, when the Old Dominion marked the second anniversary of another set of executions. These put to death twenty-seven perpetrators of Gabriel's rebellion, an aborted revolt that involved blacks from no fewer than ten counties and came closer to toppling the Virginia slave system than any such uprising before or since.

The dilution of white blood would compromise the existing political order.

Slave insurrections made white southerners anxious, not only about the maintenance of their monopoly on power but also about the purity of their race. If blacks craved white freedom, they thought, then blacks also craved white mates. The dilution of white blood would compromise the existing political order; it would result in confusion, chaos, and, eventually, in the diminution of white liberty.[10] This understood, the meaning of Callender's charges becomes clear. If Jefferson retired to his private chambers with Hemings, he violated the promise of an all-white and entirely free America.

AN UNRELIABLE NARRATOR

Yet Callender's volley of opprobrium missed its mark. In October, at the same time reports of "dusky Sally" filled Federalist papers, John Quincy Adams decried the president's "democratic popularity" and moaned that "the strength of the present administration is continually increasing." Callender's efforts to impugn the president foundered both above and below the Mason-Dixon line, among Federalists and Republicans alike. His reputation as an erratic, spitfire polemicist sharply curtailed his effectiveness with northerners, many of whom not only smirked at his depiction of Jefferson but also had difficulty regarding with seriousness anything that came from his pen. "I believe nothing that Callender said, any more than if it had been said by an infernal spirit," John Adams wrote in 1810. "I would not convict a dog of killing a sheep upon the testimony of two such witnesses." Federalist printers who wished to maintain their credibility could not embrace the journalist's account without equivocation.

No matter how "convincing" printers of the *Connecticut Courant* claimed to find Callender's tale, his record as a scandalmongering, partisan hatchet man could have done little to persuade readers of his accusation's veracity. Under threat of arrest by British authorities for seditious libel, Callender had fled to America in 1793, where he soon took up his pen in opposition to what he viewed as Federalist corruption. He authored pamphlets, wrote prolifically for Republican prints, and earned the scorn of prominent Hamiltonians such as Theodore Sedgwick,

Callender's record as a scandalmonger undermined his accusation.

Samuel Dexter, Harrison Otis, Robert Goodloe Harper, and fellow newspaperman John Fenno, who described him in 1798 as a "wretch" entitled "to the benefit of the gallows." Stung by his criticisms, voluminous and venomous, Callender's enemies struck back. Judge Samuel Chase, an ardent Federalist, fined and imprisoned Callender in 1800 for violation of the Adams administration's sedition law. For years, Federalists had smeared Callender's reputation and attacked his integrity. Now that he had switched sides in the political struggle, how could they best make use of his claims against Jefferson and still save face?[11]

By the time the *Recorder* went to press with its report on miscegenation at Monticello—complete with a James T. Callender by-line—newspapers of the Federalist persuasion had already reprinted several installments of a *New-York Evening Post* series titled "Jefferson & Callender." Damning the president for his contributions of money and advice to the polemicist, the series sought to cast doubt upon Jefferson's patriotism by calling attention to claims made by Callender in his latest manifesto, *The Prospect Before Us*. The pamphlet, which Jefferson was said to have reviewed before publication, contained "an open attack on the Federal constitution, and unqualified abuse of Gen. Washington, and of his [successor in] the Presidency, Mr. Adams, besides slander on other eminent and virtuous Federal characters," according to one of the pieces in the *Post*. Quoting from his *Prospect*, the newspaper spotlighted Callender's contention that the Constitution was "cram[m]ed down the gullet of *America*," his belief that every "Virginian who values his freedom . . . should perfect himself in the use of the musket" in preparation for battle with the federal army, and his disdain for the "Monarchs of Braintree and Mount Vernon." The *Columbian Centinel* printed a letter that called Callender's polemic an "*infamous* and *disgusting* publication." A few issues later, the *Centinel*'s publisher quoted from Jefferson's correspondence with the Scot: "I thank you for the proof sheets you inclosed me, such papers cannot fail to produce the best effect." The Federalists scored points against Jefferson, but they also savaged the reputation of the man who had now turned against him.

Unable to convincingly refurbish Callender's authority and unwilling to ignore his assault on the president, Federalist newsmen seized upon their one remaining alternative. They reprinted or repeated the *Recorder*'s accounts of Jefferson's miscegenation, sowing the seeds of scandal while avoiding the appearance of hypocrisy by reminding readers of Callender's supposed penchant for fabrication. One *Gazette of the United States* writer, for example, reiterated the Sally Hemings story, but then piously maintained that "as we possess no positive vouchers for the truth of the narrative, we do not choose to admit it into the Gazette while there remains a possibility of its being a calumny." The *Connecticut Courant*, before reprinting the *Recorder*'s account, reported to readers that "J. T. Callender, who wrote and laboured to overthrow the administrations of Washington and Adams, has turned his artillery against Mr. Jefferson." The Federalist prints' duplicity regarding the contentious polemicist did not escape notice. As a delegate from Worcester noted several years later on the floor of the Massachusetts House of Representatives, "in one breath they call Callender the greatest liar that ever existed, and in the next produce him as their witness."[12]

The president's opponents circulated the charges, but failed to expand on them. Callender ran out of rumors to repeat, and most Republican journals denied his charges a printed response. Federalists seized on the few replies to the Hemings story as opportunities to prolong the public's exposure to the issue. When one Jeffersonian penman angrily denounced Callender's "*damnable lie*" and warned that indignant citizens might reward the "outcast" with bodily harm, the *Recorder* reprinted the tirade in full. Antiadministration prints, in fact, tried to bait Jefferson's supporters. If the allegation against the commander-in-chief's character "is not true it will doubtless be contradicted by proper authority," averred one writer. Another pointed toward the "silent confession of the democratic prints." Callender himself goaded his former allies. "If the friends of Mr. Jefferson are convinced of his innocence, they will make an appeal of the same sort. If they rest in silence," he contended, "they cannot hope for credit. The allegation is of a nature too black to be suffered to remain in suspense." Despite the Federalists' entreaties, only a few of the president's allies hazarded rebuttals.[13]

RACE-MIXING AND WHITE SUPREMACY

In the South, Republican reticence served not only to quiet the rumors but also to salve any anxieties that Callender's report provoked among the slaveholding elite. Many planters must have doubted the story; all who paid attention to the partisan press understood that the journalist who propagated the account would go to great lengths — and perhaps even lie — to diminish his enemies in the eyes of the public. Still, more than a handful of slaveholders, themselves keepers of black concubines, must have found the idea of Jefferson acting in the same manner far from inconceivable. But the behavior of the president, who stood accused of endangering white supremacy, confirmed that he did nothing to place it in jeopardy.

Ethics below the Mason-Dixon line tolerated race-mixing under certain circumstances but rejected it in others. Working-class whites found guilty of fornicating with free blacks often faced severe retribution. The child of a white and a free black was a free mulatto and, as many citizens thought, a likely recruit for dangerous revolutionaries such as Gabriel. Thus Callender printed one article in the series about "Sally, and President Tom" under the headline "Free Negroes."

He failed to recognize, however, that planters could philander with slaves without fear of serious consequences because the child of a slave and her master was still only a slave. This double standard made sense. So long as southerners abided by a certain set of unwritten rules, their actions did not imperil the balance of racial power.[14]

But this slave-based society prescribed more for planters than the mere maintenance of their mistresses and mulatto children as chattel. Whites also had to act discreetly; according to Bertram Wyatt-Brown, when their trysts came under scrutiny, the only acceptable response was stoic and silent denial. In addition, the "relationship, even if long-standing, had to seem to be a casual one in which the disparity of rank and race between the partners was quite clear to any observer." The affair, moreover, "could not be part of a general pattern of dissoluteness. If the wayward white was alcoholic, unsociable, and derelict about civic duty or work, then his keeping a mistress became a subject of general complaint." Finally, "the concubine had to be sexually attractive in white men's eyes. The lighter the skin, the more comely the shape, the more satisfactory the arrangement appeared to be."[15]

Callender and his journalist allies ineffectually accused the president of breaking this code of conduct. They laced with sarcasm their descriptions of Sally, the "African Venus" and "copper coloured charmer" who supposedly caused Jefferson to abandon the antimiscegenation arguments spelled out in his *Notes on the State of Virginia* and "to have laid aside all his fear about the 'beauty' of our race, suffering by a 'mixture' with the other." In addition, Callender claimed, his "yellow son" did not know his place, for this "young MULATTO PRESIDENT" had begun "to give himself a great number of airs of importance in Charlottesville, and the neighborhood." Such reports smacked of satire. They could hardly rebut the testimony of Jefferson's own actions or cast doubt on the understanding that his behavior fully complied with the standards of his native South. If Jefferson lifted his slave onto his bed, he did nothing to elevate her within society. Accused of miscegenation, the polymath master of Monticello could not be charged with indolence. Physical descriptions of Hemings, if taken literally, bestowed on her the beauty of a "Venus." Finally, Jefferson's cool-headed disregard for the charges indicated that he maintained firm control over his passions, his slaves, and himself.

Anxieties over intermixture in this era of black rebellion neither resulted from nor responded to the supposed situation at Monticello because they had little connection with plantation miscegenation. The *Recorder* remarked that "the country would no longer be habitable" if every white man in Virginia followed Jefferson's example and fathered five mixed-race children. But mulattoes born into slavery posed much less of a threat than the prospect of a burgeoning population of free mulattoes—the products of relationships between whites and free blacks. In practice, even proven affairs between white masters and their black paramours did little to damage planters' reputations. Master-slave adultery, in and of itself, seldom served as grounds for divorce, and while aristocratic matrons bemoaned the undeniable practice of plantation miscegenation, their husbands turned deaf ears. Slaveholders continued to sire mulattoes until the Civil War destroyed their peculiar institution. Callender may have observed apprehensions over black uprisings, but he was blind to the subtleties of the southern psyche.[16]

Revelations of private sins mattered less than public crimes.

PRIVATE TRESPASS, PUBLIC OFFICE

Just as an uneven grasp of southern racial anxiety caused the journalist to miss his target, his imperfect understanding of what Americans demanded from officeholders blunted his attack. Revelations of unseemly personal deeds among men in prominent posts titillated newspaper readers, but many citizens—maybe most—cared more that their leaders faithfully executed official duties. This fact Callender should have comprehended, for a recent controversy in which he had involved himself strongly suggested that revelations of private sins mattered less than public crimes. Five years prior to the publication of the Hemings story and before the journalist had turned his back on the Republican cause, Callender printed rumors that Alexander Hamilton had abused his office, become involved with a reprobate character named James Reynolds, and joined him in a shady scheme of speculation with government funds.

Hamilton, in turn, issued a printed response designed to show that he had violated his own marital vows but not the public's trust. "The charge against me," he recounted in a pamphlet, "is a connection with one James Reynolds for purposes of improper pecuniary speculation. My real crime is an amorous connection with his wife." In 1791, he confessed, serving in Philadelphia as secretary of the treasury while his wife and children spent the summer in their native New York, he had "frequent meetings" with Maria Reynolds. Their first encounter took place in her bedroom; most subsequent rendezvous occurred at his own place of residence. "The intercourse with Mrs. Reynolds . . . continued," Hamilton admitted, even after it became apparent that her husband knew of their affair and would use it to blackmail him. James Reynolds initially sought compensation through appointment to office. But Hamilton, although thoroughly seduced by Maria's artful affections and "tender" love letters, could not bring himself to place "private gratification" above "the public interest." Instead of a job on the government payroll, he offered Reynolds $1,000 of his own money. This payment preceded a string of loans and contributions that for a few months bought Maria's services and her husband's silence.

Contrary to the "vile" accusation of Callender, Hamilton countered, pecuniary speculation had never entered into the sordid triangle of lust, seduction, and extortion. It was a personal affair of passion, not an official act of treachery. But it was also the wellspring of a rumor that placed Hamilton in a no-win situation. To ignore Callender's charge would leave allegations of official misdeeds unanswered. To hazard an honest response, however, would expose private infidelities by entering them into the public record. "Even at so great an expense," Hamilton wrote, the "disagreeable embarrassments" sure to result from his choice of the latter option might "wipe away a more serious stain."

Hamilton believed that the public viewed marital malpractice as less egregious than official wrongdoing. Politicians might commit errors in their private lives, he thought, but only mistakes made in public capacities could end their careers. Although Republican papers made merry with recountings of Hamilton's extramarital amours for more than a year, even after public revelation of the Reynolds affair, he remained as a possible candidate for office, humiliated personally but vindicated politically.[17]

Benjamin Franklin, George Washington, and Jefferson all survived accusations of improper sexual conduct with white women. In 1763 a young Pennsylvanian reported to a friend the "generally Known" fact that Franklin had fathered an illegitimate son. It hardly mattered, however, because the "happy Qualities with which G[overno]r F—k—n is possessed and the Good he may do in his Sphere of Action. . . . has already overcome the Prejudices of the People so much that his Governorship probably will be easy and prosperous." Likewise, Revolutionary War-era rumors spread by loyalist propagandists that Washington kept a battlefield mistress did little to diminish his reputation as a stalwart defender of his nation's honor.[18]

Such was the same for Jefferson, whom Callender accused not only of lusting after a slave but also of pursuing the affections of a married white woman. While the veracity of the former charge remains uncertain, the truthfulness of the second indictment is indisputable. In 1768 a bachelor Jefferson unsuccessfully sought the sexual charms of Betsy Walker, the wife of his friend and neighbor John Walker. By the 1790s, after politics drove a wedge between the two men, rumors of the attempted affair began to circulate. In 1802 they became public when Callender aired them shortly after he made his allegations concerning Hemings. Even before the journalist put details of the Walker involvement in print, others in the press alluded to Jefferson's clumsy venture into extramarital intrigue. A writer for the *Columbian Centinel* noted Callender's tale of miscegenation at Monticello, but then added that there existed "a story, *the truth of which WE DO KNOW*, of a much more criminal and flagitious transaction than the one of which the President is accused." Jefferson had once attempted adultery, the writer implied, and had been "forced out" of the woman's house "with an insulted husband's foot at his crapper." A subsequent account held that Betsy Walker herself had repelled Jefferson, and not with a kick but with a pair of scissors.

It made sense for contemporaries to brand Jefferson's youthful pursuit of his friend's wife "more criminal and flagitious" than his alleged romps with an "African Venus." Betsy Walker belonged to another man, according to the ethic of the time, but "Black Sal" belonged to him. In attempting to seduce Walker, Jefferson endangered the sanctity of her legally recognized marriage and cast aside his own honor-bound friendship with her husband, with whom he shared memories of their years together as schoolboys. Hemings, on the other hand, existed as his personal property. Given the dehumanizing views of blacks held by many citizens, to make her his concubine could be no more egregious than to indulge in a peculiar form of self-gratification. An affair with Hemings would be an unsavory but purely personal act. His attempted affair with Walker revealed a more serious flaw in his character, however, because it signified a disregard for fraternal loyalty and the rights of his peers.[19]

Not surprisingly, Callender's charge regarding the Walker incident reverberated more strongly than the Hemings story, and it more successfully goaded responses both from Jefferson's followers and from Jefferson himself. Early in 1805 the *New England Palladium* repeated the Walker story in considerable detail and then made cursory reference to the "sable damsel" to whom Jefferson supposedly turned after receiving his friend's wife's rebuke. One of the newspaper's printers later noted the relative unimportance of the Hemings charge, explaining that "the person in question was a domestic, a part of his property." When Republicans in the Massachusetts House of Representatives advanced a resolution calling for their state to break a printing contract with the *Palladium*'s owners, they virtually ignored the president's slave and, like the newspaper, focused their attention on the publication of the Walker incident. Edgy and indignant, they insisted that the journal stepped out of bounds because it impugned an official for an act of no public importance. Significantly, an opponent of the measure argued along similar lines. "Why," asked a representative from Brookfield, "should the House trouble itself as to the [newspaper's] offence . . . against the *private* character of Mr. Jefferson?" The charge against the president—acting improperly outside of his official capacity and before his term in office began—had no relevance to the public. "Whether the resolution" against the *Palladium* "was approved, or negatived," a legislator predicted, the allegation "would not hurt Mr. Jefferson's reputation." John Leland, a Baptist preacher who once lived near Monticello, agreed. He had "never heard a syllable" spoken of either rumor, he said, and neither mattered, for Jefferson's "public administration has been just and economical."

But a claim that Jefferson misused his presidential influence in order to suppress damaging testimony about his sexual past did matter, and it constituted the final notable aftershock of Callender's accusations. In 1806 the Republican-controlled Connecticut circuit court indicted Reverend Azel Backus for seditious libel, alleging that he had called Jefferson "a liar, whoremaster, debaucher, drunkard, gambler, and infidel" who procured from his slaves "a wench as his whore." Through a friend, however, Jefferson communicated to the court that "if the tenor of my life did not support my character, the verdict of a jury would hardly do it." Because, he said, of his sympathies for the feelings of the Walker family, he hoped for the case to be dropped. After some delay, the court acceded to his request. Although papers publicized the clergyman's alleged remarks, not a single direct reference to Hemings appeared in print during the episode; even the *Connecticut Courant*, which a few years earlier had eagerly propagated Callender's rumor, now described Backus's charges against Jefferson as "unfounded."[20]

One Federalist pamphleteer calling himself "Hampden" learned of the president's involvement in the case's dismissal, however, and he argued that "the only opportunity that ever did, *or ever will occur*, of proving before a court and jury the *chaste* attempts of Mr. Jefferson upon the wife of his friend," had been "superseded *by Mr. Jefferson himself!*" He reminded readers that the president's oath of office bound him "to take care that the law be faithfully executed" and charged him with obstruction of justice. These serious allegations consumed the bulk of the pamphlet, and apparently the author saw neither a need nor felt an inclination to comment on the substance of Backus's remarks about Jefferson's "whore." There was a difference between personal and political behavior, as even Callender conceded. "The world has no business" with the private element "of a public character," he said, "unless . . . it shall be connected with some interesting political truth."

But some, like Callender, thought that Jefferson's private life revealed much about his conduct as an officeholder. If a couple of members of the Massachusetts assembly believed that the stories of Walker and Hemings had little to do with his capacity to manage the government, others said that "the preservation of our Republican Constitutions, and the impartial and faithful administration of laws enacted in conformity to them, depend alone on the knowledge which the people may have of the *conduct, integrity and talents* of those of their fellow citizens, who have been, or may be called to offices of trust and honour." As a member of the Massachusetts legislature maintained in a response to an 1803 speech by governor Caleb Strong about a different issue, a polity would go to ruin "if a sentiment should prevail, that public virtue and private vice are compatible qualities in the same character, that licentiousness and profligacy are no objections in candidates for public office."[21] If these assertions represented a conviction among some that personal failings mirrored public behavior—for example, that Jefferson's purported affair with a woman of African descent was inconsistent with the views expressed about interracial relationships in his *Notes* and exemplified a gen-

eral pattern of hypocrisy—they could not convince all. For the many Americans who had no desire to find reasons to spurn Jefferson, such precepts counted for little; they had already imbibed perfectly palatable justifications for ignoring Callender's tale.

"LONG FORGOTTEN ANECDOTES"

The Sally Hemings scandal gave Americans who opposed Jefferson no reason to embrace him, but it also failed to convince supporters that he should be abandoned. Callender's impact on the political landscape was to produce a tremor and not an earthquake. Charges of miscegenation may have caused some to doubt the wholesomeness of Jefferson's personal life, but they did not convince everyone, nor did they succeed in ruining the president's reputation. An increasing majority of Americans viewed the leader of their nation as a man of wisdom, honor, and benevolence. Four months after Callender launched his attacks, Joseph Priestly, a British-born theologian, wrote that Jefferson's "administration is, indeed, excellent, highly favourable to the peace and happiness of the country in all respects." After all, he said, "all the internal taxes are abolished" and "a great proportion of the national debt was discharged the last year." Even some of the people who considered Jefferson's personal behavior remained unconvinced that it was anything but exemplary. At a Massachusetts banquet celebrating Jefferson's second inauguration, for example, a man toasted the president, "the *purity* of whose private character, adds *lustre* to his public virtues." A few months later, at a Philadelphia Fourth of July banquet, diners raised their glasses to Jefferson: "May his name hereafter be as a monument for public and private example." A woman from Louisville named Elize Winn, moreover, regarded Jefferson as the "Father of the nations, our emperor, the man we love." Her faith in his fidelity did not equivocate. "You are all thats [*sic*] good and god like," she told him in an 1803 letter.

For all these individuals, steamy stories of Jefferson's supposed affair with a slave had scant credibility and even less relevance. Callender, who soon after the Hemings controversy drowned first in liquor and then in the shallow waters of the James River, seemed irregular, volatile, and untrustworthy. The fact that he authored the essays impugning Jefferson did nothing to enhance their believability. Nor did Jefferson's reticence, which regularly characterized his responses to attacks. Even if the tale of plantation passion were true, the master of Monticello behaved in the manner expected of a gentleman, doing nothing to undermine white hegemony in Virginia's multiracial society or, according to some, Americans' trust in his ability to administer their government. In short, those who sought reasons to disbelieve or disregard the story found many of them.

This pleased John Adams. Although his party stood to gain from the perpetuation of the rumors regarding Jefferson's private life, such tales, he contended, would do nothing to advance the "public good." Little more than eight years after Callender issued his allegations concerning Jefferson's attempted seduction of Walker and his reputed affair with Hemings, Adams described the accounts as "long forgotten anecdotes" best consigned to obscurity.[22]

NOTES

The author presented an earlier draft of this essay at the 1995 annual meeting of the Society for Historians of the Early American Republic. For critical challenges and encouragement, he wishes to thank William Howard Adams, Douglas Egerton, Joseph Ellis, Annette Gordon-Reed, Peter Onuf, Herbert Sloan, Lucia Stanton, Harry Watson, Joel Williamson, Douglas Wilson and, especially, Don Higginbotham.

1. Advertisement in *The National Intelligencer and Washington Advertiser*, 18 August 1802; 25 August dispatch from Richmond, in the *Columbian Centinel* (Boston), 4 September 1802; *The Recorder: or Lady's and Gentleman's Miscellany* (Richmond), reprinted in the *Connecticut Courant* (Hartford), 10 September 1802 and 27 September 1802.

2. Michael Durey, *"With the Hammer of Truth": James Thomson Callender and America's Early National Heroes* (University Press of Virginia, 1990), 143–49; *Gazette of the United States* (Philadelphia), 7 September 1802; *Connecticut Courant*, 10 September 1802.

3. Jefferson to Dr. George Logan, 20 June 1816, in Paul Leicester Ford, ed., *The Works of Thomas Jefferson*, 12 vols. (G. P. Putnam's Sons, 1904–5), 11: 527.

4. A number of scholars find implausible the idea of a sexual relationship between Jefferson and Hemings, but Annette Gordon-Reed's *Thomas Jefferson and Sally Hemings: An American Controversy* (University Press of Virginia, 1997) shows that many of their arguments suffer from flawed analysis.

5. See Sidney Press Moss and Carolyn Moss, "The Jefferson Miscegenation Legend in British Travel Books," *Journal of the Early Republic*, 7 (1987): 253–74; [Thomas Green Fessenden], *Democracy Unveiled; or, Tyranny Stripped of the Garb of Patriotism, by Christopher Caustic, L.L.D.* (Boston, 1805), 104–8; [William Cullen Bryant], *The Embargo, or Sketches of the Times; A Satire* (Boston, 1808), 7; John Quincy Adams, "The Discoveries of Captain Lewis," *Boston Review and Monthly Anthology*, 4 (1807): 143–44. On the 1802 elections, see Noble E. Cunningham, Jr., *The Jeffersonian Republicans in Power: Party Operations, 1801–1809* (University of North Carolina Press, 1963), 71.

6. *Recorder*, reprinted in the *Connecticut Courant*, 10 September 1802; *Lynchburg Gazette*, reprinted in the *Recorder*, 3 November 1802; *Columbian Centinel* (Boston), 15 September 1802; Virginius Dabney, *The Jefferson Scandals: A Rebuttal* (Dodd, Mead, 1981), 10–11, 13 (quotations); "A Philosophic Love-Song, To Sally," *Boston Gazette*, reprinted in the *Port Folio* (Philadelphia), 6 November 1802; *Recorder*, reprinted in the *Gazette of the United States*, 7 September 1802, 22 September 1802.

7. John Adams to Col. [Joseph] Ward, 8 January 1810, John Adams Letterbook, Massachusetts Historical Society, Boston, microfilm reel 118; David Rice, "Slavery Inconsistent With Justice and Good Policy," [1792] in Charles S. Hyneman and Donald S. Lutz, eds., *American Political Writing During the Founding Era, 1760–1805*, 2 vols. (Liberty Press, 1983) 2: 874. On miscegenation in the South, see John W. Blassingame, *The Slave Community: Plantation Life in the Antebellum South*, 2nd ed. (Oxford University Press, 1979), 154–56; John D'Emilio and Estelle B. Freedman, *Intimate Matters: A History of Sexuality in America* (Harper & Row, 1988), 102–3; Eugene D. Genovese, *Roll, Jordan, Roll: The World the Slaves Made* (Pantheon, 1972), 423; Thelma Jennings, " 'Us Colored Women Had to Go Through a Plenty,': Sexual Exploitation of African-American Slave Women," *Journal of Women's History*, 1 (1990): 60–66, 72–74; Kenneth M. Stampp, *The Peculiar Institution: Slavery in the Ante-Bellum South* (Knopf, 1956), 359–60; Joel Williamson, *New People: Miscegenation and Mulattoes in the United States* (Free Press, 1980), 42–43; Henry Bibb, *Narrative of the Life and Adventures of Henry Bibb, An American Slave* (New York, 1849), 112–18.

8. Jefferson, *Notes on the State of Virginia*, ed. William Peden (1785; University of North Carolina Press, 1954), 138, 141, 143; Jefferson to William Short, 18 January 1826, in Ford, ed., *Writings of Thomas Jefferson*, 10: 362; James Sullivan to Dr. Jeremy Belknap, 30 July 1795, "Queries Relating to Slavery in Massachusetts," in *The Belknap Papers*, 2 vols. (Boston, 1877–1891), 2: 414; Winthrop D. Jordan, *White Over Black: American Attitudes Toward the Negro, 1550–1812* (University of North Carolina Press, 1968), 545 (quotation). See also David H. Fowler, "Northern Attitudes Toward Interracial Marriage: Legislation and Public Opinion in the Middle Atlantic States and the States of the Old Northwest, 1780–1930" (Ph.D. diss., Yale University, 1963), 84–95. On the lineage of the Hemingses, see Dumas Malone, *Jefferson and His Time*, 6 vols. (Little, Brown, 1948–81), 4: 495, and Williamson, *New People*, 43–44.

9. Thomas Dwight to Hannah Dwight, 24 October 1803, Dwight-Howard Papers, Massachusetts Historical Society, Boston; *Frederick-Town Herald* (Maryland), reprinted in the *Gazette of the United States*, 27 September 1802; *New-York Evening Post*, 30 December 1801. On Federalist criticisms of Jefferson's inconsistent stands on equality and slavery, see Linda K. Kerber, *Federalists in Dissent: Imagery and Ideology in Jeffersonian America* (Cornell University Press, 1970), 27, 39, 51–52.

10. Douglas R. Egerton, *Gabriel's Rebellion: The Virginia Slave Conspiracies of 1800 and 1802* (University of North Carolina Press, 1993), 141, 145, 186, 68; Durey, *"With the Hammer of Truth"*, 137–39; Jordan, *White Over Black*, 470, 578–82.

11. John Quincy Adams to Rufus King, 8 October 1802, in Charles R. King, ed., *The Life and Correspondence of Rufus King*, 6 vols. (New York, 1896), 4: 176–77; Adams to Ward, 8 January 1810, John Adams Letterbook, microfilm reel 118; Durey, *"With the Hammer of Truth"*, 44–47, 53–109,

129–35; *Gazette of the United States*, 27 April 1798; James Morton Smith, *Freedom's Fetters: The Alien and Sedition Laws and American Civil Liberties* (Cornell University Press, 1956), 342–56.

12. Durey, *"With the Hammer of Truth"*, 113, 117, 119–20; "Jefferson & Callender, No. 10," *New-York Evening Post*, reprinted in the *Columbian Centinel*, 21 August 1802; 28 August letter from Philadelphia, *ibid.*, 4 September 1802; Jefferson to Callender, 6 October 1799, excerpt published in *ibid.*, 16 October 1802; *Gazette of the United States*, 7 September 1802; *Connecticut Courant*, 10 September 1802; "Legislature of Massachusetts, House of Representatives: Thursday, Jan. 31, 1805, DEBATE on Mr. Allen's Resolution for dismissing the Printers of the PALLADIUM," *Columbian Centinel*, 9 February 1805.

13. "A Friend to Good Government, From the Republican Watch Tower, For the American Citizen," *Recorder*, 29 September 1802; *Gazette of the United States*, 7 September 1802; *Frederick-Town Herald*, reprinted in *Gazette of the United States*, 27 September 1802; *Recorder*, reprinted in *Connecticut Courant*, 10 September 1802.

14. "Free Negroes," *Recorder*, 10 November 1802; Egerton, *Gabriel's Rebellion*, 166–67; Robert McColley, *Slavery and Jeffersonian Virginia*, 2nd ed. (University of Illinois Press, 1973), 111; John H. Russell, *The Free Negro in Virginia, 1619–1865* (Johns Hopkins University Press, 1913), 64–65, 69, 131, 167–68; Stampp, *Peculiar Institution*, 353; John Taylor, *Arator: Being a Series of Agricultural Essays, Practical and Political: In Sixty-Four Numbers*, ed. M. E. Bradford (1818; Liberty Classics, 1977), 115.

15. Bertram Wyatt-Brown, *Southern Honor: Ethics and Behavior in the Old South* (Oxford University Press, 1982), 307–8; Catherine Clinton, *The Plantation Mistress: Woman's World in the Old South* (Pantheon, 1982), 211, 214. Apparently, despite his stated opposition to miscegenation, even Jefferson could turn a blind eye to it in practice. Thomas Bell, a Charlottesville merchant whom Jefferson described as "a man remarkable for his integrity," first leased and then purchased from Jefferson Mary Hemings, with whom he admitted to having fathered two children. See Lucia C. Stanton, " 'Those Who Labor For My Happiness': Thomas Jefferson and His Slaves," in Peter S. Onuf, ed., *Jeffersonian Legacies* (University Press of Virginia, 1993), 170, 173.

16. *Frederick-Town Herald*, reprinted in *Gazette of the United States*, 27 September 1802; *Recorder*, reprinted in *Gazette of the United States*, 7 September 1802; *Recorder*, 22 September 1802; Wyatt-Brown, *Southern Honor*, 307, 289.

17. The pamphlet, *Observations on Certain Documents Contained in No. V & VI of "The History of the United States for the Year 1796," In Which the Charge of Speculation Against Alexander Hamilton, Late Secretary of the Treasury, is Fully Refuted. Written by Himself* (Philadelphia, 1797), is reprinted under the heading, "Printed Version of the 'Reynolds Pamphlet'," in Harold C. Syrett, *et al.*, eds., *The Papers of Alexander Hamilton*, 27 vols. (Columbia University Press, 1961–87), 21: 238–85, 243, 244, 249, 251, 252 (quotations); Forest McDonald, *Alexander Hamilton: A Biography* (Norton, 1979), 227–30, 237, 243–44, 258–59, 286, 334–36; Broadus Mitchell, *Alexander Hamilton*, 2 vols. (Macmillan, 1957–62), 2: 139, 169, 209, 217, 399–422, 457, 486, 504; John C. Miller, *Alexander Hamilton: Portrait in Paradox* (Harper, 1959), 333–40, 458–59, 462–64, 485–86. Miller maintains, however, that Hamilton's pamphlet did little to reverse the ill effect of Callender's attack because it "persuaded few Republicans that he was innocent of financial wrongdoing" (464).

18. George Roberts to Robert Crafton, 9 October 1763, extracted in Leonard W. Labaree, *et al.*, eds., *The Papers of Benjamin Franklin*, 32 vols. to date (Yale University Press, 1959–present), 11: 370–71; John C. Fitzpatrick, *The George Washington Scandals* (Mount Vernon Ladies Association, 1929).

19. *Columbian Centinel*, 15 September 1802; "Federal Misperception Detected, No. XXIV," *National Intelligencer*, 29 September 1802; Malone, *Jefferson and His Time*, 1: 42, 57, 59, 153–54.

20. "The Monarchy of Federalism," *New England Palladium* (Boston), 18 January 1805; *ibid.*, 25 January 1805; *ibid.*, 31 January 1805; [Alexander Young], *The Defense of Young and Minns, Printers to the State, Before the Committee of the House of Representatives; With an Appendix, Containing the Debate, &c*, (Boston, 1805), 14–15; "Legislature of Massachusetts, House of Representatives: Thursday, Jan. 31, 1805, DEBATE on Mr. Allen's Resolution for dismissing the Printers of the PALLADI-UM," *Columbian Centinel*, 9 February 1805; L. F. Greene, ed., *The Writings of the late Elder John Leland* (New York, 1845), 286; Leonard W. Levy, *Jefferson & Civil Liberties: The Darker Side*, 2nd ed. (Quadrangle, 1973), 61–66; Malone, *Jefferson and His Time*, 5: 373, 378–79, 386–91; Jefferson to James Madison, 25 August 1807, in James Morton Smith, ed., *The Republic of Letters: The Correspondence Between Thomas Jefferson and James Madison, 1776–1826*, 3 vols. (Norton, 1995) 3: 1491–92; *Connecticut Courant*, 30 September 1807.

21. "Hampden" [David Daggett], *A Letter to the President of the United States, Touching the Prosecutions, Under His Patronage, Before the Circuit Court in the District of Connecticut* (New Haven, Conn., 1808), iv, 5, 17, 18, 20, 26–27; Durey, *"With the Hammer of Truth"*, 94 (quotation); *Defence of Young and Minns, Printers to the State, Before the Committee of the House of Representatives* (Boston, 1805), preface; "Answer to the Governor's Speech, Jan. 23, 1805," *Columbian Centinel*, 26 January 1805. Jan Lewis and Jacob Katz Cogan present excellent discussions of these competing modes of thought in their respective essays, "The Blessings of Domestic Society," in Onuf, ed., *Jeffersonian Legacies*, esp. 121–28, and "The Reynolds Affair and the Politics of Character," *Journal of the Early Republic* 16 (1996): 389–417. I view analysis of the importance of public officials' private characters for this period as a classic half-full/half-empty debate. Although Lewis and Cogan argue that, on balance, citizens cared deeply about an officeholder's reputed moral fiber in nonpublic matters, I contend that in Jefferson's case, at least, they did not.

22. Joseph Priestly to Theophilus Lindsey, 1 January 1803, Original Letters from Dr. Joseph Priestly, Dr. Williams's Library, London; Unidentified newspaper clippings, documenting a 4 March 1805 banquet in Charlestown, Massachusetts and a 4 July 1805 banquet in Philadelphia, in "The Jefferson Family Scrapbooks," vol. 2 of 3, Manuscripts Department, University of Virginia, Charlottesville; Elize Winn to Jefferson, 20 February 1803, in Jack L. McLaughlin, ed., *To His Excellency Thomas Jefferson: Letters to a President* (Norton, 1991), 136; Adams to Ward, 8 January 1810, John Adams Letterbooks, microfilm reel 118.

The Great Wagon Road, or How History Knocked the Professor Cold, or A Storyteller's Story, or Why Appalachians Are Mountains and a People

by Michael Chitwood

In "The Great Wagon Road," published in the Spring 1997 issue of *Southern Cultures*, historian T. H. Breen told of his encounters and adventures while attempting to trace the route of the great migration of German and Scotch-Irish settlers from lands north into the Carolinas. Breen's essay set Michael Chitwood to thinking . . .

Scottish, by way of Ulster, Philadelphia,
the Valley of the Shenandoah,

generous, clannish, violent, kind-hearted,
they walked in (the Germans rode)

and stayed mostly out of county records
and the backs of Bibles, unlettered.

Their only correspondence with me,
son of their children's children's great grandchildren,

is this ditch, these nearly healed wheel cuts,
the line they traced in the earth.

. . . .

Locally, it took its name from where it was going,
the potent away-from-here, the better place,

the how-it-could-be, not wintering on beans,
the infant not dead with the flux,

the ground not snagged with roots
that sang from the plow's cut and welted the shins.

Yonder. Chewed with scratch biscuits,
smoked in the porch shade.

Something to be believed
when believing was the only solace.

. . . .

"Fortunately, only Single Brothers
made this trip. This trail

at times is impassable and these folk
are wild, unpredictable.

Unlike our brethren,
they came not seeking but fleeing,

the almshouse, the sheriff,
a shamed woman or her brothers.

We sought the freedom to worship.
They worshipped freedom from seeking."

. . . .

"I don't know now, though I knew. . . ."
Her palsied hand goes to her forehead

as if to draw memory with a touch.
My past grows dim,

illiterate, abandoned,
free for the taking.

. . . .

A boy of four, he killed
one of the King's overlords

for casting a desirous eye on his mother,
and stowed away to sail the whale road.

Saving the crew and cargo from storm,
he was rewarded in Philadelphia

with a seventeen-hand stallion
and rode out of the city stench

to the Blue Ridge which reminded him of home.
There he killed and married Cherokee,

fathered seven sons and seven daughters,
coaxed Highland pipes from fiddle's catgut,

distilled moonlight, slaughtered hogs,
lost fingers in sawmills,

hoed, suckered, topped and primed tobacco
discarded washing machines in creekbeds,

learned to read the Bible, believe obituaries
and recite where he was and what he was doing

when the first Ford, radio, television
and news of JFK's death arrived.

He put on a tie, conditioned the air
and forgot the song of the whippoorwill.

....

"There is not history, but histories."
His shoes aren't right for the rough ground.

The sapling branches whip his back
as he backs into where we're going.

Educated, tenured, he hopes to publish
a study of The Great Wagon Road.

"Until documented the facts are in flux."
He is lecturing backward into the understory

where a honeysuckle vine catches his heel.
He barks his bald spot on a sweet gum

and is silenced into the fact of himself.
Out cold, he's received his dissertation's introduction.

....

Count Casimir Pulaski, Bishop
Francis Asbury, Lorenzo Dow,

the Moravian Single Brother who wrote
"We had to watch our horses closely. . . ."

They crossed the Maggodee, Blackwater,
and Pigg, scribbled down some thoughts

that I'm stealing outright,
keeping an eye on their horses, too.

Warrior's Trace, gospel road, going now
into sumac, scrub pine and books,

somewhere along the way I got your dirt
in my shoes, and that will do.

reviews

Our regular review section features some of the best new books, films, and sound recordings in southern studies. From time to time, you'll also find reviews of important new museum exhibitions and public history sites, and retrospectives on classic works that continue to shape our understanding of the region and its people. Our aim is to explore the rich diversity of southern life and the methods and approaches of those who study it. Please write us to share your suggestions, or to add your name to our reviewer file.

The Power of the Porch

The Storyteller's Craft in Zora Neale Hurston,
Gloria Naylor, and Randall Kenan
By Trudier Harris
Mercer University Lamar Memorial Lectures,
No. 39
University of Georgia Press, 1996
xiv, 152 pp. Cloth, $22.95

Reviewed by **Margaret D. Bauer**, assistant
professor of southern literature in the English
Department at East Carolina University. She recently
assumed editorship of the *North Carolina Literary
Review*. Her publications include essays on Hurston,
William Faulkner, Alice Walker, Ellen Gilchrist,
Kate Chopin, Ellen Glasgow, Margaret Mitchell, and
Mark Twain.

In her preface to this collection of her 1995 Lamar Memorial Lectures, Harris explains that, upon first being invited to give the lectures, she knew immediately that she wanted to speak on the "orality" of Zora Neale Hurston's work. Her selection of Hurston's *Mules and Men* points to the value of Harris's volume of essays: *The Power of the Porch* provides detailed explorations of previously neglected works. Though there is a body of criticism on *Mules and Men*, it is dwarfed by the available commentary on *Their Eyes Were Watching God*. Harris's other chapters examine more recent works that have not yet received much critical analysis (Naylor's *Mama Day*) or any critical analysis at all (Kenan's "Clarence and the Dead"). Readers of Naylor and Kenan will therefore be pleased to see these works receiving Harris's scrutiny.

Harris examines Hurston's many roles in *Mules and Men*: compiler, frame narrator, audience, and character. To assemble this collection of folktales from the citizens of her native Eatonville, Florida, Hurston had to win her former neighbors' trust, sometimes by convincing them that she was one of them and that she had not been changed by city life and education, at other times by playing the part, often flirtatiously, of helpless, even potentially victimized female. Always, Harris points out, Hurston was as aware of her intended audience as she was of the people who provided her subject matter. Thus she sometimes feigned ignorance to elicit explanations of customs or tales in the same vernacular in which they were introduced. Harris points out the inconsistency of Hurston's dual roles of insider and naïf and suggests that the ability to handle this contradiction was one of her great talents. Equally with the storytellers she recorded, Hurston was a "Performing Persona" (the title of Harris's section on *Mules and Men*).

Also representative of the author's role-playing talents, according to Harris, is the way that Hurston used notions of traditional femininity and her own sexuality to coerce men to talk: she baked for them, flirted with them, or allowed them to "rescue" her. Thus, although Harris asks readers to be wary of applying contemporary feminist ideology to a work published in 1935 (which would result in criticism of the sexism in many of the stories and of the author herself for not commenting on it), her suggestion of Hurston's masking provides something of an answer to this paradox.

Harris's discussion of the various roles that Hurston played in *Mules and Men* also illuminates the author's achievements with similarly complex narration in *Their Eyes Were Watching God*, which begins with Janie telling her story to Phoebe, but then slips into a third-person narrative voice that at times speaks in standard English and at other times in dialect. Thus Harris provides implicit support for the argument that Hurston's narration is purposeful rather than inconsistent or merely sloppy.

In the last part of her discussion of *Mules and Men*, Harris turns to Hurston's voodoo tales, providing a smooth transition to the central focus of her subsequent lectures on the supernatural elements in *Mama Day* and "Clarence and the Dead." In her preface, Harris announces a goal of moving readers toward acceptance of such "features in African American culture that their rationalist minds might have wanted to reject." It is an aim she believes she shares with the writers of these works, for she links the orality of these narratives to their authors' common desire to win over their audiences and convince them of the value of the respective cultures depicted in their works. Thus, in these discussions Harris again connects the orality of the texts, reflected in the first person "we" of the respective narrative voices, with audience awareness. The comforting voice of a storyteller soothes the reader into accepting the fantastic tales.

As the reader of Charles Chesnutt's conjure tales will know, significant truths can be learned from seemingly incredible stories—that is, if one does not dismiss the possibility of truth because of prejudice toward that which does not comply with one's own concept of reality. As I followed Harris's very rational exploration of the supernatural occurrences in *Mama Day* and "Clarence and the Dead," which omits question of the believability of these events, I was reminded of Gay Wilentz's article on Toni Morrison's *Song of Solomon* (in *African American Review*, 1992). That essay challenges a reader who might jump to the conclusion that Milkman's final "flight" is suicide because people can't fly. The character is, after all, a descendent of flying Africans; denying his ability to fly, then, is a rejection of his cultural heritage. When I pose Wilentz's question, "whether Milkman dies or flies," to my students, I ask them to compare the legend of flying Africans to a pretty incredible legend that most of them accept without question: the legend of Jesus rising from the dead. What is the difference between these legends other than the cultures out of which each seemingly impossible feat emerges? Harris seems to be asking readers of Hurston, Naylor, and Kenan for a similar acceptance of another culture's beliefs that Wilentz asks of Morrison's readers.

In her preface Harris mentions another of Kenan's recurrent themes: the conflict between homosexuality and traditional Christianity, but she includes only a brief reference to "The Foundations of the Earth," in which Kenan discussed this conflict perhaps most poignantly. Similarly, Harris mentions other controversial subjects in his work before proceeding to his use of the supernatural. Thus, Harris's chapter on Kenan, while it provides a close reading of only one story, still introduces this new writer to readers who may be approaching his work for the first time.

....

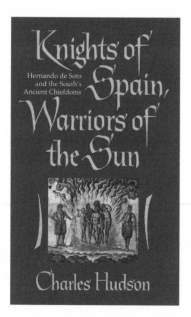

Knights of Spain, Warriors of the Sun

Hernando de Soto and the
South's Ancient Chiefdoms
By Charles Hudson
University of Georgia Press, 1997
559 pp. Cloth, $34.95

Reviewed by **Peter H. Wood**, professor of early American history at Duke University, where he regularly teaches courses on colonial history and Native American history. His article on the French explorer La Salle appeared in the April 1984 issue of the *American Historical Review*.

In 1847 while debate over the controversial War with Mexico raged in Congress, the decoration of Charles Bulfinch's U.S. Capitol Building was nearing completion. John Trumbull's four epic scenes of the revolutionary era had graced one side of the massive Rotunda for several decades, and three paintings featuring Columbus, Pocahontas, and the Pilgrims had recently been added. At last a congressional committee, attentive to sectional divisions, selected an Ohio artist to depict a Deep South scene with implications for westward expansion: William H. Powell would portray the *Discovery of the Mississippi by De Soto, A.D. 1541*. The finished painting showed the Spanish explorer on a white horse, flanked by a heavy cannon and a massive cross, accepting the submission of feathered Indians huddled before western-style teepees. By the time Powell's symbolic image of De Soto was finally installed in 1854, the self-made adventurer was becoming a permanent feature in the American pantheon of Christian explorers/founders.

Part of the era's fascination with De Soto and the narratives of his sixteenth-century *entrada* sprang from the exploration of ancient Indian mounds by newcomers to the Mississippi Valley. For instance, one such amateur archaeologist, Dr. M. W. Dickeson, teamed with artist J. J. Egan in 1850 to create a continuous painting, more than 7 feet high and nearly 350 feet long, displaying dramatic scenes from the region, past and present, which could be unfurled before paying customers. A century later, as a small boy growing up in St. Louis, I watched this same *Mississippi Panorama* unwind once again in a captivating museum exhibit in 1949. More than the images of tornadoes, steamboats, or "Dr. Dickeson Excavating a Mound," the scene I recall most vividly (and which engaged the imagination of a six-year-old with a fascination of early southern history) was entitled "The Burial of De Soto." It depicted loyal followers secretly lowering the body of their leader into the Mississippi by moonlight in May 1542, so that local Indians would not learn of his death.

Little happened between 1850 and 1950 to change America's vague and positive mythic image of the empire-seeker who had first risen to fame as an aggressive participant in Pizarro's conquest of the Incas in Peru. As the De Soto expedition's four-hundredth anniversary approached in 1938, a government-sponsored commission, headed by Smithsonian anthropologist John R. Swanton, published an elaborate but speculative report on the Spaniard's much-debated path, and schoolchildren dutifully traced his supposed route onto outline maps of the Southeast. But the epoch in which he lived, and the worlds through which his invading army traveled, remained totally obscure in a region that piously marked its colonial beginning with the English settlement of Jamestown in 1607. Over the past half-century, however, numerous forces have conspired to alter this entrenched pattern, and at last we are beginning to obtain a broader and more complex picture of De Soto and his times.

Southern archaeology has grown rapidly in scope and sophistication in recent decades, particularly with regard to the early post-contact era following the arrival of Europeans and Africans. Among American historians, scholars of the colonial era have gradually shown an increasing awareness of the Deep South and of non-English colonization. Simultaneously, experts on Hispanic America have again stretched northward beyond Mexico and the Caribbean to explore what Herbert Bolton called "the Spanish Borderlands." So when David J. Weber recently published *The Spanish Frontier in North America*, the book's dust jacket still carried Powell's romantic painting of De Soto, but its contents showed how far the scholarship has progressed. It is appropriate that Weber's splendid survey appeared in 1992, for the five-hundredth anniversary of Columbus prompted extensive reexamination of the "lost sixteenth century." All of these forces have helped to foster a diverse group of southern "ethnohistorians"—interdisciplinary researchers at home with the methods of history and anthropology.

Many of these energetic scholars have concentrated on the sixteenth century, and for nearly twenty years a small band, led by anthropologist Charles Hudson of the University of Georgia, has focused on understanding the complex details and implications of the De Soto story. "I realized that if one could reconstruct the activities of this expedition accurately enough," Hudson writes, "it would become possible to link this information together with a considerable body of information archaeologists had been collecting for over a century." Not only would this yield a new "picture of the social geography of the sixteenth-century Southeast," but it would also become possible for the first time "to examine how the sixteenth-century native societies had evolved from earlier antecedents and to proceed forward in time to show how this 1539–43 Southeastern world gave way, fell apart, and reorganized itself into the peoples of the eighteenth-century South."

As these scholars deciphered parts of the puzzle, they presented their findings, first in articles and then in books. In 1993 Hudson teamed with Jerald T. Milanich to publish *Hernando de Soto and the Indians of Florida*. The following year, with Carmen Chaves Tesser, he edited *The Forgotten Centuries: Indians and Europeans in the American South, 1521–1704*. Now Hudson (whose 1976 text, *The Southeastern Indians*, remains a standard in the field) has produced the culmination of his protracted studies, a volume recounting the brutal narrative of the Spanish expedition and the equally absorbing and varied responses of the Native Americans they encountered. At one level the book is reminiscent of Herbert Bolton's 1949 biography of De Soto's contemporary, *Coronado: Knight of Pueblos and Plains*. But Hudson pays particular attention to precise geography and to the varied southern forests of a distant era, so I am also reminded of the valued edition of William Bartram's *Travels*, edited by naturalist Francis Harper in 1958.

"My desire for this book," Hudson states at the outset, "is that it evoke the sixteenth-century Southeast and make it palpable, not only in words but also in illustrations." Using clear prose and nearly a hundred detailed maps and pictures, he succeeds admirably in his appointed task, giving us the best single-volume narrative to date of the fateful and ill-fated Spanish expedition that chopped and pillaged its way across the southern interior between 1539 and 1543. His opening chapter, "Separate Worlds," gives a succinct introduction to sixteenth-century Spain and to Native American societies on the eve of contact. Chapter two provides a balanced overview of De Soto's remarkable life. Hudson's final chapter summarizes the differing after-effects of the invasion for Spanish and Indian survivors. "For the native chiefdoms of the Southeast," he concludes bluntly, "the De Soto expedition was an unimaginable calamity." An extended afterword conveys well the historiographical complexities that bedevil a thoughtful interdisciplinary study such as this.

The sixteen intervening chapters, which make up the heart of the book, follow the expedition from its arrival in 1539 at Tampa Bay with a force of well over six hundred, until the survivors, scarcely half that number, pass down the lower Mississippi in seven crude open boats and skirt the Gulf Coast to Mexico in the summer of 1543. Hudson's citations are extensive, but he generously confines to the footnotes most scholarly debate about the location of specific sites and the viability of competing texts, so that we are drawn into the harrowing drama of this extended cultural confrontation. Readers who have been taught to distrust the "black legend" of Spanish cruelty will no doubt be surprised by the use of attack dogs to kill local inhabitants, just as readers inclined to see early Indians as passive and peace-loving farmers will be jolted by the incessant warfare that divides regional chiefdoms. More than once the huge and novel horses of the Spanish are offset by the accurate and powerful arrows of the native bowmen.

Writing about exploration and cultural conflict presents peculiar challenges. Limited and conflicting European accounts, created by persons whose cultural and geographical notions were flawed at best, must be matched up with scant and contested archaeological and linguistic data. Then, generations of secondary assessments, many of them deeply biased and flawed, must be sifted and compared. Finally, all the competing and contradictory claims of contemporary scholars, politicians, and local pot hunters and boosters must be reconciled or rejected. De Soto's march through the South, like the marches of Cornwallis and Sherman in later centuries, will remain a topic of fascination and controversy for years to come, but Charles Hudson's masterful new book has raised the level of the discussion for all who will come after him, and he has made an invaluable contribution to the historical understanding of Native American life in the Southeast.

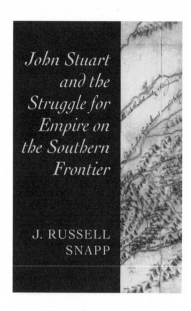

John Stuart and the Struggle for Empire on the Southern Frontier

By J. Russell Snapp
Louisiana State University Press, 1996
238 pp. Cloth, $42.50

Reviewed by **Robert M. Weir**, professor of history at the University of South Carolina and the author of *Colonial South Carolina: A History*.

J. Russell Snapp's volume joins a rapidly lengthening list of new studies of the southern frontier in the eighteenth century—all intent on enlarging our understanding of Native Americans, Indian-white relations, and/or the American Revolution in the region. Insofar as it shares these aims, Snapp's volume is not unique, but to my knowledge no other recent author has offered such a direct challenge to a work that has long been considered standard in the field.

In 1944 John Alden's *John Stuart and the Southern Colonial Frontier: A Study of Indian Relations, War, Trade, and Land Problems in the Southern Wilderness, 1754–1775* covered much of the same ground over a shorter chronological period and concluded that Stuart's outstanding traits as superintendent of Indian Affairs of the Southern District of North America were "fidelity and prudence." In summary, Alden observed, "his conduct of Indian affairs in the South before the American Revolution must be regarded as a bright spot in the uneven record of British administration of the American colonies in the later eighteenth century." Snapp's volume, on the other hand, takes the story into the early nineteenth century. "Thanks to officials like Stuart," he argues, "no middle ground apparently existed between acceptance of thoroughgoing British rule and complete American independence" because his program revealed "a fateful obliviousness to the political and social perspectives of still-powerful creole colonists."

Snapp develops this argument in interesting ways. During the first part of the eighteenth century, he contends, veteran merchant-traders gained considerable influence with the Indians of the Southeast and used this influence to maintain order and stability in the region. After mid-century, however, new men arrived, bent on land acquisition and/or trade with the Native Americans, and their proliferation threatened the established arrangements. John Stuart, appointed Indian superintendent for the Southern District in 1762, responded by attempting to instill centralized "order and regularity." But his efforts appeared to be coupled with favoritism toward his fellow Scotsmen, and they restricted the autonomy of the old traders and the provincial figures with whom they were linked. Stuart therefore inspired hostility toward himself, his Scottish brethren, and other "outsiders" who seemed to be favored by imperial authorities. Receiving less consistent support from his British superiors than from Native American leaders, who feared American encroachment, Stuart found that his ability to implement plans for centralized control of Indian affairs reached its peak only after the Revolution had begun. But his use of influence to mobilize the Indians against the American rebels alienated potential Loyalists and inflamed inveterate Whigs. The results manifested themselves in alignments that persisted well into the nineteenth century. From Florida, Spanish authorities and Scottish merchants supported the southeastern Indians in the hope of limiting the expansion of the United States; Americans, with the help of state governments, and later the United States itself under Andrew Jackson, successfully sought the removal of the Native Americans, in one way or another. Furthermore, memories of outside interference with local control of Indian affairs helped to make southerners hypersensitive on the subject of any outside meddling.

This argument has much to commend it. That elites resented meddling in their governing of local affairs was clearly the case in many areas. Furthermore, Indian relations were obviously very important to the security of the southern colonies. Some southerners were manifestly expansionist, which brought them into conflict with Stuart, who sought to protect Native Americans and their territorial claims. Thus the general parameters of the local situation make the author's argument plausible; the difficulties arise with some of the details. For example, if his view is correct, established Indian traders and territorial expansionists in the southern colonies should have been early and ardent Revolutionaries as a result of their conflicts with Stuart. A few indeed were; but some of the most important figures were late and reluctant rebels, while several individuals with whom Stuart clashed were Loyalists. Moreover, the most important institutional voice of the elites whose activities Stuart presumably thwarted came from the lower houses of the local assemblies. To judge from the evidence presented in this volume, these houses were comparatively indifferent to Stuart's activities. If this was in fact the case, it requires explanation. To be entirely convincing the author needs to discuss these and similar questions at greater length.

Finally, and perhaps most interestingly, Snapp's argument not only challenges Alden's interpretation of Stuart's role, but it also runs counter to the thrust of much of the recent scholarship in the field, which tends to be sympathetic to Native Americans. Thus Snapp's condemnation of Stuart for impeding the aspirations of white colonials risks appearing more dated than Alden's earlier praise of Stuart's responsible efforts to protect the Indians. Snapp is aware of this pitfall and, in general, skirts it with considerable agility. Stuart's not entirely unalloyed good intentions receive appropriately qualified praise, while his supposedly clumsy attempts to implement them incur criticism. But sustaining these distinctions would seem to require demonstration that there was a viable middle ground—that colonial expansionism and the protection of the Native Americans were in the final analysis compatible and that Stuart could have done a better job of reconciling these apparently conflicting ends. Snapp argues unconvincingly for a middle way. Still, the author is to be commended for both his intellectual independence and his nuanced presentation of an extended essay that is stimulating as well as challenging.

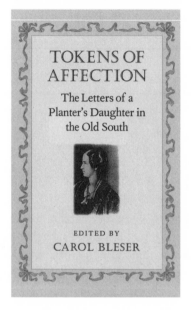

Tokens of Affection

The Letters of a Planter's Daughter
in the Old South
Edited by Carol Bleser
University of Georgia Press, 1996
403 pp. Cloth, $45.00

Reviewed by **Jane Turner Censer**, professor in the Department of History at George Mason University. Censer recently edited and wrote an introduction to a novel about Reconstruction, *Like unto Like*, written by Sherwood Bonner in 1878 and republished by the University of South Carolina Press in its "Southern Classics" series.

In her introduction to *Tokens of Affection,* Carol Bleser alludes to the spell that Maria Bryan's letters cast over John Shaw Billings II, managing editor of *Time* magazine and Henry Luce's second in command. In the 1950s Billings would sometimes hurry home from meetings just to spend the evening perusing letters written by Maria Bryan, his great aunt who had been dead over a century. Why were these letters so compelling to him and why are they still interesting today?

On its face this correspondence does not fit the usual description of an entertaining set of letters. Some readers enjoy letter writers who knew charismatic, powerful individuals, visited exotic locales, or participated in major events such as the Civil War. Other collections attract readers because they depict a two-way conversation that was a lively intellectual exchange. Yet other letters hold interest because they detail the spiritual, intellectual, or political growth of the writer. This set of letters conforms to none of those typical patterns. Nevertheless, many readers will find themselves agreeing with Billings, a shrewd businessman and newspaperman, that these letters are fascinating.

The attraction comes from Maria's skill at recounting and describing the events of her rather circumscribed world—that of planter society in early nineteenth-century Georgia. Maria was a close observer and an inveterate raconteur, chronicling with humor and affection the foibles of her society. Carol Bleser aptly compares the letters to the delicately wrought miniature portraits so popular at the time.

Maria Bryan Harford Connell lived a relatively short, uneventful life. Born in 1808 to a planter family in Hancock County, Georgia, she married twice, never had children, and died at age thirty-six. Her closest long-term relationship seems to have been with her beloved older sister Julia. When Julia married Henry Cumings and went to live in Augusta, the devoted sisters bridged their separation with chatty letters. Maria, perhaps because she had cautioned Julia to burn all her letters, wrote frankly and at length about all the activities of their family and friends. In a rural community, a letter writer such as Maria could depend on such staple topics as church affairs, courtships and marriages, births, illnesses, and deaths, with a sprinkling of business news and social occurrences.

Maria delights the modern reader with the tableaus she presented in her letters to Julia. Some of these were wonderful anecdotes replete with deftly sketched characters and dialogue, as when Maria, on a trip to visit relatives in the North, met in a train station "a lady of very stylish appearance" who refused to pay a fare for the poodle accompanying her. Maria then trouped in a wide cast of supporting personnel who participated in the disagreement, which at one point threatened to erupt into a full-scale melee. Despite Maria's fascination with romantic novels of the day, she shares in rural wit as she remarks about one friend's suitors, "I think she will have taken her pigs to a poor market if she accepts either of these gentlemen."

At other times, Maria's letters chronicle an ongoing saga featuring her family and neighbors. Maria's correspondence with her sister lasted almost twenty years, long enough to see many changes in their lives and situations. Making frequent appearances was Maria's older brother Joseph, who was prone to ill-fated courtships and sullen disagreements with his parents. The Old South presented few alternatives for young men of good family—planting, medicine, law, the church—and Joseph was one of those young men who struggled to find a profession. Trained as a lawyer, young Joseph Bryan had little talent or inclination for it; yet his interest in farming was at best minimal. At times he seemed to be trying to strike a Byronic pose: "Joe, you know, never speaks unless, like a ghost, he is first spoken to." Indeed, even after the reader loses sight of him, at Maria's death, Joseph remained a young man adrift. Also in the letters, younger sister Sophia grows from a school girl into a young woman whose flippancy and lack of religious sentiment at times bewilder the more conventionally religious Maria.

Yet Maria for all her chattiness shows a cool reserve in regard to her own affairs. She veils much of her own story, including the events that led up to each of her marriages, the first a union of which her parents apparently did not approve. Thus, the reader is surprised when the letter writer almost laughingly records a neighbor's judgment of herself: "'Maria,' said she, 'is a very good girl—but I think she courts attention rather too much.'" Amidst the terseness and reserve, Maria does admit some of the trials of womanhood that she experienced. Throughout much of her life, Maria was the dutiful daughter who tried to smooth family relations. After her first husband's death, she returned to live with her parents and strove for the resignation that her Presbyterian piety and even her beloved sister enjoined upon her. There she cheerfully taught her nieces and nephews and took on the responsibilities of managing that household after the death of her mother.

In the end she found the life of a southern matron hard. Upset when the overseer beat a slave, leaving her face "bloody and swelled," Maria told her sister "Oh! how great an evil is slavery." Yet in that case, as with her father's desires to migrate westward, Maria apparently saw herself as unable to exercise power over male decisions. Similarly, she only hints at the unhappiness that editor Bleser believes existed in the second marriage. Neither confessional nor self-justifying, Maria Bryan's letters are a window onto her society and help to build a complex and nuanced understanding of women's roles in it. They carry us back to a small world full of its own tragedies and triumphs.

....

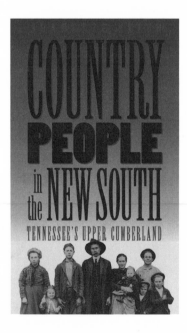

Country People in the New South

Tennessee's Upper Cumberland
By Jeanette Keith
University of North Carolina Press, 1995
xi + 293 pp. Cloth, $45; paper, $18.95

Reviewed by **Michael Lienesch**, Bowman and Gordon Gray Professor of Political Science at the University of North Carolina at Chapel Hill. Lienesch is the author of *New Order of the Ages: Time, the Constitution, and the Making of Modern American Political Thought* and *Redeeming America: Piety and Politics in the New Christian Right*. He is currently at work on a study of the political causes and consequences of the Scopes "monkey" trial.

As southern cultures go, we may know least about the largest: the millions of rural white people, many of them poor, whom Frank Owsley called "plain folk." Historically they have been an elusive population: celebrated by Jeffersonians as sturdy and virtuous yeomen, denigrated by conservative elites as "crackers" or "rednecks," embraced by progressives as backward victims of an oppressive social system and by populists as heroic protesters against it. But especially in the twentieth century, poor rural whites all too often have been forgotten or at least pushed to the margins of the picture, portrayed as the people who remained when others moved to the Sunbelt cities and suburbs. In the New South, they are the ones, to use Hal Baron's phrase, "who stayed behind."

In her thoughtful and thought-provoking *Country People in the New South*, Jeanette Keith describes some of these plain folk and discusses some of the ways they responded to the changing character of southern society at the beginning of the twentieth century. Her focus is on the Upper Cumberland, a region of eleven counties in northeastern middle Tennessee between Nashville and Knoxville that consists mostly of hill country, much of it divided by steep-sided ridges and shallow rivers. The land has always been poor, capable of producing field crops and some tobacco, but unsuitable for plantation production. Even in the late nineteenth century, when Keith takes up her study, the area remained sparsely settled, primarily by poor whites who lived on farms along the creeks and at the crests of the ridges, or in tiny crossroads towns with names like Difficult and Defiance. They lived in crude cabins or simple frame houses, usually without indoor plumbing and sometimes not even an outhouse. Most of them were not educated beyond the fifth grade; some had not traveled as far as the county seat.

Keith describes these country people with care and considerable sensitivity, steering clear of both stereotypes and nostalgia. Her scholarly task is by no means simple, since her subjects, often articulate but usually not very literate, left little in the way of diaries or letters. But by using a variety of sources, including local and state records, small town newspaper reports, and some oral histories, she has pieced together a clear and compelling picture of their lives.

The Upper Cumberland was ruled by patriarchs who fathered large families, expected back-breaking work from their wives, and controlled their children by keeping them close to home. These poor white farmers resisted authorities and refused to pay taxes, told their preachers and teachers what to preach and teach, and settled disputes on their own, often with armed kinfolk at their side. Today they would be seen as backward and primitive people, or possibly as picturesque. But Keith treats them realistically and respectfully; taking them on their own terms, she lays out the logic of their lives: avoiding debt, reducing risk by relying on their families, controlling their communities, assuring the salvation of their souls.

The book follows these country people of the Upper Cumberland through a time of transition, from approximately 1890 to 1925, when railroads began to reach into the region, bringing with them not only banks and businessmen but also a contingent of progressive reformers. In a series of chapters, Keith describes the conflicts that developed when poor farmers resisted these business progressives in their campaigns to bring better roads, schools, and civic institutions into the backcountry. The best of the chapters recounts what may have been the biggest battle of the day, the struggle to reform the rural schools. It tells how as late as 1900, common schools in the Upper Cumberland consisted of one-room buildings in which poorly trained—sometimes barely literate—teachers led classes for three months out of the year. Attendance was not compulsory and therefore sporadic. No county had its own high school, and none was needed, since most students had dropped out by the fifth grade. For their part, country folk seemed happy with the situation, since better schools would encourage students to look beyond the boundaries of their family farms and perhaps even leave for the cities. So when educational progressives appeared with their plans for longer school terms, graded classes, professional teachers, and public high schools—all to be run by county superintendents and town-controlled boards of education—rural communities used all of their resources to prevent and subvert these reforms. By the 1920s, schools in the region were only slightly better, and even with compulsory education, most children still dropped out before completing the eighth grade.

In these and other struggles, Keith finds that neither side exactly won. For although the reformers were able to bring about some changes, especially in building roads, country folk proved remarkably adept at protecting their culture by adapting, co-opting, and flat-out rejecting other reforms. Even World War I, during which progressive elites took control of war mobilization efforts, did not provide the reformers with victory on the home front. Many hill men resisted conscription or even deserted, feeling more loyalty to their families and their pacifist religious views than to a nation they knew little about and a jingoistic nationalism that failed to resonate with their daily lives. And at the close of the war, with the resurgence of conservative values in the 1920s, the traditionalists found their opposition to modernism to be almost in the mainstream. So it was that when state representative J. W. Butler of Macon County, an Upper Cumberland farmer himself, sponsored the anti-evolution bill that would lead to the Scopes trial, he was able to assert a brand of conservative public religion that appealed not only to the Tennessee country folk who were his neighbors but to millions of others, especially in the South, who were searching for security in a rapidly changing world.

Keith's choice to conclude her narrative in 1925 with Butler and his anti-evolution bill is convenient but arbitrary. For as she shows, the consequences of the region's resistance to progress extended far beyond the 1920s. In an epilogue, she mentions some of her own memories of growing up in the Upper Cumberland of the mid-twentieth century, describing a region of failing farms and declining employment in which the mostly female workforce was employed in low-wage, non-union plants, working for few benefits and with little hope of advancement. Even in the 1990s, she finds that local schools remain poor, and that less than half of all adults have a high school education. The conclusion she draws is inescapable: that by refusing to invest in a future they could not imagine, the people of the Upper Cumberland paid the price of condemning their children to poverty. Sadly, it is a price that all too many country people in the New South continue to pay.

....

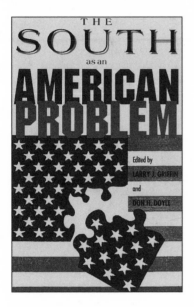

The South as an American Problem

Edited by Larry J. Griffin and Don H. Doyle
University of Georgia Press, 1995
310 pp. Cloth, $30.00

Reviewed by **Peter A. Coclanis**, George and Alice Welsh Professor of History at the University of North Carolina at Chapel Hill and author of *The Shadow of a Dream: Economic Life and Death in the South Carolina Low Country, 1670–1920*.

In writing this review, I promised myself I would not start by alluding to a collection of essays on the South written almost seventy years ago by a dozen intellectuals associated with Vanderbilt University. Just because the new collection, *The South as an American Problem*, is the work of a dozen writers associated (more or less) with Vanderbilt University was no reason to take such a stand—or so I thought. But, alas, there is no getting around it: Although *The South as an American Problem* is not organized as tightly as the famous Fugitive/Agrarian manifesto of 1930, it covers enough of the same ground to invite comparison, as Larry J. Griffin and Don H. Doyle, the editors of the newer collection, readily acknowledge.

To say that the Griffin-Doyle collection shares some of the same ground with its illustrious predecessor, *I'll Take My Stand*, is not to suggest that it espouses the same "agrarian" values, advances the same "anti-industrial" and "anti-modern" arguments, or assumes the same rhetorical tone. Rather, *The South as an American Problem*, which grew out of an interdisciplinary faculty seminar at Vanderbilt during the 1992–1993 academic year, shares a concern with southern identity, broadly conceived, and an interest in the problematic relationship between the South and the polity of which it is part, the United States. Although the various contributors to the Griffin-Doyle collection—six historians, two literature professors, one sociologist, an economist, a legal scholar, and a journalist—fail to agree on either the nature of southern identity or the particular problem posed by the South to the United States, they do converse with and play off of one another in extremely interesting ways. No manifesto, then, but manifest and manifold virtues nonetheless!

Perhaps the single most impressive virtue of this collection is its intellectual subtlety, particularly in "problematizing" topics ranging from climate to culture, and from slavery and secession to the rise of the sunbelt. After a brief introduction, coeditor Larry Griffin, for example, opens with an essay that probes the very idea of a southern "problem," demonstrating that the definition of the problem has shifted markedly over time. Griffin suggests in his provocative conclusion that America has always needed a problematic South in order to grasp and occasionally to confront and overcome broader American ills. None of the other contributors operates on the same lofty (and abstract) plane as Griffin, a distinguished sociologist, but each at once enriches as he/she revises our understanding of individual "problems" in, about, or relating to the South.

On our descent from Griffin's opening essay, we first encounter David L. Carlton's brilliant piece on the ways in which the economic culture of the South came to diverge from that of the nation as a whole in the nineteenth century. Joyce E. Chaplin's insightful and often surprising essay on the "problem" of southern climate details whence this problem arose and how it changed over time. Chaplin's essay is followed by four strong pieces on race relations in the South (including slavery) at various points in time, by James Oakes, Don H. Doyle, James W. Ely Jr., and Hugh Davis Graham. The last of these essays—on the successes and ironies of the so-called Second Reconstruction—is especially commendable in my view.

Economist Robert A. Margo weighs in next with an incisive essay wherein he challenges conventional notions about the performance of the southern economy over time, particularly the notion that the region stagnated economically in the period between 1880 and 1940. Literary scholar Eric J. Sundquist follows with a powerful critique of Harper Lee's *To Kill a Mockingbird*, the withering nature of which is modulated by the next essay: Jimmie Lewis Franklin's elegiac meditation on southern identity.

Literary historian Michael Kreyling follows with an assessment of both the power and the limits of critic Louis Rubin's vision of the South. The volume concludes with a balanced but, ultimately, upbeat little essay by journalist John Egerton on the South's tortuous history and the progress the region has made in recent years.

The South as an American Problem is a superb volume that deserves a broad readership. If it is any indication of the state of southern studies at Vanderbilt today, the "twelve southerners" who published that earlier collection in 1930 could not but concede, however grudgingly, that the field is in excellent, if ideologically different hands.

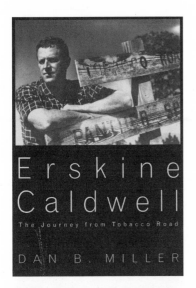

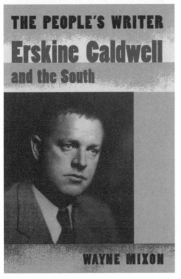

Erskine Caldwell

The Journey from Tobacco Road
By Dan B. Miller
Alfred A. Knopf, 1995
459 pp. Cloth, $30.00

The People's Writer

Erskine Caldwell and the South
By Wayne Mixon
University Press of Virginia, 1995
213 pp. Cloth, $27.50

Reviewed by **Bryant Simon**, assistant professor in the Department of History at the University of Georgia.

Last year, I assigned Erskine Caldwell's *Tobacco Road* to my upper-level twentieth-century U.S. history class. On the first day of the quarter, as the students scanned the syllabus, one of them asked, "Who is this Erskine Caldwell guy?" I answered with a question, "Have any of you heard of Erskine Caldwell?" Only one woman out of the thirty or so in the class—most of them from Caldwell's native Georgia—raised her hand. She said she thought that he wrote "dirty, crude" books. I informed the class that Caldwell was one of the most popular writers in American history, and that in the 1960s he was dubbed "The World's Best-Selling Novelist." I told them that a stage version of *Tobacco Road* was the second longest running Broadway drama of all time. Just as I was about to rattle off another Caldwell fact, one of the students interrupted me and demanded, "Well, if he's so popular, why don't we know anything about him?"

Considered for years by many to be too vulgar, too commercial, and too critical of the South, Caldwell was first dismissed and then forgotten. Even his most probing novels, *Tobacco Road* and *God's Little Acre*, were eventually ignored. By the time of his death in 1987, most of his 25 novels, dozen nonfiction books, and 150 short stories were out of print. Over the last several years, however, something of a Caldwell revival has started to take shape. The University of Georgia Press has brought many of his books back into print. Scholars, meanwhile, have begun to seriously reexamine Caldwell's life and work. Historians Dan Miller and Wayne Mixon are two of the central figures in this Caldwell renaissance, and their recently published books have helped to resuscitate Caldwell as an important literary and historical figure.

Remarkably, Miller's book, published in 1995, is only the second full-scale biography of Caldwell—a man who sold more than 70 million books. Relying on a wide array of sources, including interviews with Caldwell family members and the entire, voluminous Caldwell collection at Dartmouth College, Miller traces the Georgia-born writer's life from cradle to grave. He is particularly interested in Caldwell's earliest influences, most notably Caldwell's father, Ira. An ordained minister, the iconoclastic Ira Caldwell was committed to helping the poor regardless of color or creed. His brand of the Social Gospel often put him at odds with his typically conservative, white supremacist neighbors. "As an adult," Miller writes, "Erskine would make his father's cause his own, and in his writing he sought to honor and vindicate him."

Miller also documents Caldwell's circuitous path to becoming a writer with a cause. A poor student, Caldwell began writing as an undergraduate. Without a diploma, he left school to devote himself full time to his craft, but it was hard going. He received an endless stream of rejections from magazines and publishers, large and small. His personal life was troubled as well. As Miller reveals, behind the tough-guy pose that he usually struck, Caldwell really had a rather fragile psyche. He married young, and the relationship quickly turned abusive. Caldwell engaged in a series of extramarital affairs, neglected his children, and lashed out at his wife. Finally a story was published, followed by a collection of essays and a novel. As the American economy collapsed in the early 1930s, Caldwell briefly flirted with the left, but, as Miller points out, the young Georgian was never a joiner and never ideologically committed to Marxism; he was simply angry about the conditions of the poor and the callousness of the rich.

Around this time, Caldwell wrote his two most famous novels, *Tobacco Road* and *God's Little Acre*. While the frank sexuality and black humor of these books stand out, what provided their power, Miller makes clear, was that they were based on the world Caldwell knew and the people he grew up around. Making the rounds with his father, for instance, he heard about a woman who resembled the noseless, traveling evangelist Sister Bessie featured in *Tobacco Road*. Still, the characters he created in these important novels were hardly real. They were exaggerations of reality, parodies of the human tragedy of poverty and neglect. Both books were portraits of the world as it should *not* be.

Miller carefully charts the critical reception of *Tobacco Road* and *God's Little Acre*. (In fact, he does this with all of Caldwell's writing; each chapter in the biography ends with a careful juxtaposition of positive and negative reviews.) Outside the South, critics generally praised Caldwell's most compelling novels. Some even put him in the same company as the great regional realists Faulkner and Wolfe. Many southerners, however, felt betrayed by Caldwell's vision. Seeing him as a sort of literary scalawag, they attacked him and defended the region, rejecting his sexualized portrait of debauchery and dementia.

Throughout his career, notes Miller, Caldwell was obsessed with money. Critical acclaim did not immediately end Caldwell's financial problems, but it did provide new opportunities. First Broadway and then Hollywood came calling and paid him dearly for scripts and, occasionally, merely to put his name in the credits. But the real money came with the postwar explosion in paperback sales. With covers displaying scantily-clad women and barrel-chested men, Caldwell's books, good and bad alike, sold in the millions. Yet success, Miller indicates, seemed to ruin Caldwell. He went through four marriages, and at the same time, he seemed to lose his muse. According to Miller, literature became a commodity—a way to pay the bills—rather than a cherished art form or a way for Caldwell to vent his anger at poverty and injustice. As Caldwell's rage softened, his writing suffered. No longer as edgy and disturbing as *Tobacco Road* and *God's Little Acre*, his work grew repetitive, even dull. At home, meanwhile, Caldwell started to drink heavily. Miller deals with Caldwell's slow demise with sympathy and grace.

More an intellectual biography than a full-blown life history, Mixon's book nonetheless covers much of the same ground as Miller's account. Like Miller, Mixon stresses Ira Caldwell's role in shaping his son's art and sympathies. Again like Miller, he looks at Caldwell's rocky relationships with his four wives. He also charts Caldwell's literary triumphs of the 1930s and traces his commercial success and artistic decline in the 1950s (although Mixon, more than Miller, praises some of Caldwell's postwar writing.) But Mixon's real concern is Caldwell's relationship with the South and its people.

Mixon maintains that Caldwell "mounted throughout his career, an uncompromising assault on social injustice." In addition, Mixon argues that Caldwell had an "everlasting concern with the southern poor." Where some have accused Caldwell of being a traitor to his homeland, Mixon insists that he was a loyal son. The writer, he argues, loved the region enough to expose its shortcomings. Caldwell's hope, according to Mixon, was that once people recognized the problems that plagued the South—poverty, hunger, monocrop agriculture, and false piousness—they might work to correct these flaws. Even his much talked about black humor was used to heighten the horrors of southern poverty and the reaction of his audience to its many injustices. Reading between the lines of Caldwell's fiction and nonfiction, Mixon also maintains that the writer opposed the South's prevailing racial order. Some of Caldwell's most powerful characters, he points out, were African Americans who carved out for themselves lives of decency and honor from the meager resources available in the segregated South.

Furthermore, Mixon, whose praise for Caldwell is at times unrestrained, suggests that many of Caldwell's characters demonstrated agency: they were not simple victims but actors, people who shaped and made their own worlds. Yet as sympathetic as Jeeter Lester and Ty Ty Walden are, it is hard to see them as powerful figures—people capable of dictating the terms of their own lives. Instead, they seem to be functioning in a world where just about everything is stacked against them. It is a closed world with little or no way out—farming wouldn't work, going to the mills is a dead-end, religious leaders are shameless hucksters, politics is a farce, and the rich and powerful are corrupt and decadent.

Toward the end of *The People's Writer*, Mixon also deals with Caldwell's demise. While stressing some of the same issues elaborated on by Miller, he returns to his main theme—the South. Repeatedly, he insists that Caldwell's concern for the poor and the dispossessed continued unabated after World War II. What changed, Mixon opines, was that Caldwell "lost touch with the South, the source of his strength." Adrift, he was merely a writer and no longer a crusader.

Both Miller and Mixon have written excellent books, ones that should be read not just by specialists but by anyone interested in the South's past. Perhaps their greatest contribution will be to spark renewed interest in Caldwell and allow readers to discover that when he was at his best, he wrote powerful and moving stories about people who have generally been forgotten.

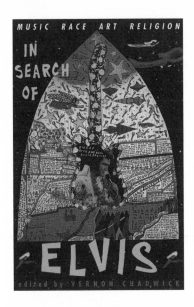

MUSIC RACE ART RELIGION

IN SEARCH OF ELVIS

edited by VERNON CHADWICK

In Search of Elvis

Music, Race, Art, Religion
Edited by Vernon Chadwick
Westview Press, 1997
294 pp. Paper, $16.50

Reviewed by **William McCranor Henderson**,
visiting assistant professor of English at North Carolina
State University. He is also a novelist (*Stark Raving
Elvis, I Killed Hemingway*), whose latest book, *I, Elvis:
Confessions of a Counterfeit King*, is a memoir of his
experiences as an Elvis impersonator.

In 1995 the highly publicized First International Conference on Elvis Presley sent a clear message: Elvis was entering the academy with all the eclectic fanfare that had made him King of Rock 'n' Roll. Though controversial, academic status for Elvis seemed appropriate, since his presence had long been felt everywhere else. But with its proximity to the long-established Faulkner Conference, which preceded it by one week at Ole Miss, there seemed to be something cheeky about the event. Hadn't one of its organizers, Vernon Chadwick, already tweaked the traditionalists by giving equal status to Elvis and Melville in a course nicknamed "Melvis"? *In Search of Elvis* is Chadwick's edition of the major proceedings of that first conference (two more conferences followed), an array of scholarly and non-scholarly presentations that manages to convey both the attractiveness of "Elvis studies" and its confusions.

This collection should go a long way toward convincing skeptics that the controversy over Elvis studies (or simply "Elvis," in quotes, as Chadwick names the symbolic totality of the subject) is based on a misunderstanding of exactly what is being studied, and to what end. After all, anyone who protests that Elvis has been raised illegitimately to Faulkner's lofty level is simply barking up the wrong tree. Faulkner may have been the infinitely greater creative artist (Elvis, after all, never even wrote a song), yet the vast influence of "Elvis" on culture—which seems to go on and on—is something Faulkner (or "Faulkner") will never come close to realizing. Joel Williamson, author of *William Faulkner and Southern History*, who is now at work on a similar study of Elvis's roots, puts the matter succinctly: "When Faulkner died, he was dead. This is not true of Elvis." Indeed, it is the "Dead Elvis" (Greil Marcus's formulation) that continues to proliferate and radiate as a potent lodestone for cultural studies and its revolutionary academic agenda—and Chadwick makes no bones about this agenda in his introduction:

"[T]he Elvis conference sounded a wake-up call to university *apparatchiks* that a new breed of educators is demanding historical, racial, class, community, and environmental accountability in the free exercise of their creative labors." *En garde*!

Chadwick also makes it clear that freewheeling textualism ("Elvis as text") and a rainbow-coalition style of liberation exegesis are the cardinal signs of his new "insurgent pedagogy." That said, it must be observed that the worst examples of this approach have an Alice-in-Wonderland pseudo-logic to them that fails to convince, since insights tend to be undercut by absurdities. In this collection, Peter Nazareth's "Elvis as Anthology" stands out as the sore thumb.

Elvis, Nazareth assumes, held political views that were consciously (if secretly) radical and activist; so he quite literally devised subtextual agendas for every artistic move he made, agendas now revealed by the sort of intellectual tea-leaf reading that is Nazareth's stock in trade. Thus the movie *Stay Away Joe* "is about neo-colonialism and the bourgeois dreams of Third World people." When Elvis stutters on "Just Because," it is "a profound political act . . . he was breaking up the imposed colonial worldview (*sic*), that is, the worldview imposed by the colonialists through their language."

"'I Feel So Bad' is about the colonial's loss of center, the center that has been taken away by colonialism." And so on. Nazareth's underlying thesis—that Elvis knowingly devised coded messages to deconstruct the imperial center—is the naked guest at the party, an assertion on the order of "Harry Truman wrote Shakespeare." Intellectual foolishness is one thing, but Nazareth's wheels spin so carelessly, fling so much data into so many bogus congruencies, that his contribution (though intermittently interesting as autobiography) comes off more as parody than real scholarship.

Fortunately, since Chadwick is committed to pulling down barriers between "experts" and the rest of us, a wide stripe of other cultural commentators is allowed in, and most of them stand on firmer ground. John Shelton Reed's conference keynote address is a revealing portrait of the local and regional social forces that produced Elvis and his family. The Depression South, he emphasizes, was a foreign country, which suggests that Elvis was almost literally an immigrant in mainstream America—something overlooked in accounts of his provincial oddities and reluctance to shed his down-home ways.

Working another side of the street, Jon Michael Spencer succeeds mostly in updating some old news: that Elvis's appropriation of "black rhythm" conveyed some revolutionary spice to rigid white sexual behavior. Bill Malone and Stephen Tucker place Elvis squarely (and accurately) in the country music and rockabilly traditions that bred him, correcting somewhat the common overemphasis on his black-gospel and blues roots. Will Campbell grapples valiantly with the appellation "redneck," trying to separate it from its pejorative association with racism and social intolerance.

A range of other viewpoints are well represented here: RCA researcher/producer Ernst Jørgensen (Denmark) and independent photo-archivist Ger Rijff testify to European fascination with Elvis and show how fan interest can translate into serious careers. (Jørgensen is largely responsible for the excellent latter-day Elvis boxed CD sets and compilations.) Collector/artist/devotee Joni Mabe describes how rampant fan-dom led to her current traveling collection of over 30,000 Elvis artifacts. Sociologist Mark Gottdiener explores Elvis as Jesus impersonator and shows how his image operates on the religious level. Primitives, such as painter Rev. Howard Finster and shrine-builder/archivist Paul MacLeod, weigh in with rambling, idiosyncratic homages to Elvis.

But Chadwick's own introductory overview is perhaps the most illuminating contribution to the volume, because it most fully suggests the exciting sweep of "Elvis" as a talismanic Excalibur—a "master key" for the study of contemporary America. If one can look beyond Nazareth's preposterousness, Elvis studies represent a rich landscape of possibilities lying relatively untouched and ready for the scholar equipped to explore it, unafraid, as it were, to pull the sword from the stone.

···

Hillbillyland

What the Movies Did to the Mountains and
What the Mountains Did to the Movies
By J. W. Williamson
University of North Carolina Press, 1995
325 pp. Cloth, $39.95; paper, $15.95

Reviewed by **James C. Wann**, composer and
performer, whose credits include Broadway's *Pump
Boys and Dinettes* and the recently filmed (for PBS)
King Mackerel & The Blues Are Running.

Some dozen years in the making, this thoroughly researched (800 films) yet highly readable treatise draws on J. W. Williamson's long-time fascination with hill-billiana, and on the long-running "Hollywood Appalachia" class he teaches at Appalachian State University in Boone, North Carolina. He knows his subject.

"My assumption is that the hillbilly mirrors us, and like most mirrors he can flatter, frighten, and humiliate. As a rough-and-ready frontiersman, he can be made to compliment American men. He can also terrify. Put him in the same woods, but make him repulsively savage, a monster of nature, and he now mirrors an undeniable possibility in American manhood. In other words, we want to be him and we want to flee him."

Davy Crockett on the one hand, and *Deliverance* on the other. On screen so many of these stories are played for laughs—Ma and Pa Kettle, early Andy Griffith, and more recently, *Raising Arizona*. Williamson's assessment of the latter: "[T]he Coen brothers who made it are snide and contemptuous at heart. But they also invented and entertained like no one else making movies in 1987 . . . *Raising Arizona* employs a screamingly funny (and absolutely deadpan) narration by Nicolas Cage as Hi, coupled with a cartoonish . . . visual style that we might call Hillbilly Reckless . . . the story mocks the sentimental Yuppie desire to achieve the ideal American family." Williamson also explores, in depth, Jesse James's many screen incarnations, the moonshine genre, and "Hillbilly Gals," among other representative characters.

Particularly fascinating is the book's section on *Thunder Road* (1958). Writes Williamson, "In the history of celluloid hillbillies, *Thunder Road* was a landmark, the first film since Biograph's *The Moonshiner* in 1904 to look at the moonshining outlaw from squarely inside the culture."

Luke Doolin, played by Robert Mitchum, who "thought up the story, produced the film, starred in it, even wrote the title song," is a moonshine runner who fought in Korea and has come home to find that the family tradition of making whiskey on their own land was now illegal. His story is "a fable about resistance, bound to fail, but brilliantly romanticized." Here is Williamson's description of a key scene:

> As Luke Doolin, Robert Mitchum lights a cigarette like a rattlesnake buzzing itself into a coil. His don't-tread-on-me potency is all the more powerful seen through the eyes of men in the audience who feel they've been trod upon. In the closing minutes of the movie, driving tight, but cool, and pursued by Lucky, the big-city henchman, Luke is overtaken on a winding mountain road. Lucky, the hired gun, pulls even with Luke and tries to muscle him off. Luke glares and Lucky glares back. Then Doolin, like a striking snake, flicks the cigarette he's been smoking through the window of the other car and into the face of Lucky, who flinches, who therefore loses, who presently dies. This is the clear, clean gesture of defiance in a dying fall, for Luke Doolin won't survive this auto race either.

The skill of Williamson's narrative portrait, with its atmospheric echoes of hard-boiled crime fiction, bolsters his critical analysis.

This analysis has its overreaching moment when Williamson, describing the car lights winding up the mountain to bring Luke's body back home, says, "The distant moving string of headlights are votive candles, for is not Luke Doolin a ritual sacrifice, the last, admirable, real man in America . . .?" More interesting is his observation that "the movie was an incredible hit in the drive-in trade . . . many a teenage hellraiser tried to duplicate the bootleg turn. Most of the ones who survived the squealing tires eventually knuckled under to the world of work and wages in the button-down, drip-dry Eisenhower years . . . mythic tragedy has a way of reasserting the status quo."

In the book's "Hillbilly Gals" section, Williamson refers to *Thelma and Louise* as the "*Thunder Road* of feminism." Respect, independence, and freedom are the issues. "For the first time, the women are allowed the full implications of their egalitarian potential, without being repossessed in every way by the close of the story." Williamson describes such repossession by revisiting *Annie Get Your Gun* (1950), *Calamity Jane* (1953), and *The Unsinkable Molly Brown* (1964). "In these musical extravaganzas, the hillbilly gal is always scapegoat and clown. In her cross-dressing, she parodies masculine power politics, openly satirizing the structure of domination, but ultimately, she succumbs to the masculine hierarchy by doffing her pants and donning a dress. All formerly free country gals eventually give up their male display (and their symbolic as well as their real independence) to become standardized wives of the most traditionally eligible male characters available. And they always give up willingly, for love. In other words, "insofar as these movies hint at a female challenge to male expectations, they are elaborate frauds and retrograde to boot."

"High concept" is a term heard often since the days of *Flashdance* and *Fatal Attraction* (come to think of it, two urban hillbilly gals—a dancing welder and a rabbit-boiling man-eater), and high concept can either "dumb down" a story (*Indecent Proposal*) or give it a zing. In the case of *Calamity Jane*, before her transformation into a dressed-up wife, there are some zingy screen moments, as described by Williamson:

> In Chicago, Calamity is first mistaken for a man on the street and is winked at by another women . . . later she finds another woman (Adelaid) Adam's maid Katie Brown, in her bustier. "Gawd Almighty! You're the prettiest thang I've ever seen! Never knew a woman could look like that!" From that point forward . . . Calamity courts Katie, even seems to marry her at one point . . . At her dilapidated cabin, Calamity's a bundle of first-night nerves. She wants so much to please Katie and Katie accepts the overture: ". . . All it needs is a woman's touch. . . ." And she paints the front door with "Calam & Katie" inscribed in a kind of lover's knot of flowers.

But shortly thereafter, "Calamity and Katie burst into a duet . . . before the song is over, we see Doris Day first in clean men's clothes and then in lacy, full ballgowns . . . Calamity becomes feminized . . . and begins her ineluctable track toward subordination as wife of Wild Bill Hickok." It would be fun to see this story with a contemporary spin sometime, in which the hillbilly gals stay together. "You is what you is what you is" said Gertrude Stein once while passing through Ellijay, Georgia. Of course, she was ahead of her time.

At the back of the book, under "Sources," are forty-three pages of notes, chapter by chapter, adding texture and evidence to the already detailed anecdotes and arguments in *Hillbillyland*. This book is likely to become a work as enduring as its popular subject.

....

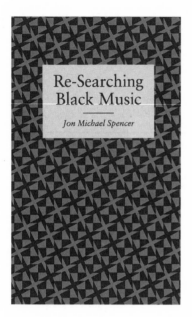

Re-Searching Black Music

By Jon Michael Spencer
The University of Tennessee Press, 1996
154 pp. Cloth, $25.00

Reviewed by **Michael Taft**, sound and image librarian and Southern Folklife Collection archivist at the University of North Carolina at Chapel Hill. He has written a number of books and articles on North American popular music, including several on African American blues.

Jon Michael Spencer's latest book may be taken as an extended introductory essay to his theory of theomusicology. His title invites us to "re-search" the subject and nature of black music; that is, Spencer asks his readers to begin again their consideration of African American musical traditions from a new, and in his opinion, fundamental standpoint—theomusicology.

Defining this standpoint takes up much of Spencer's book. He contends that religion or spirituality together with rhythm (and thereby music) are the two pillars of human society and of African American society in particular. No study of music is complete without this understanding, and all studies of music that do not acknowledge the centrality of religion are flawed. In arguing this point, Spencer shows how even the most secular forms of African American music, particularly the blues, are manifestations of the sacred, and that in fact the dichotomy between secular and sacred is a false one, that both heaven and hell are God's dominion. In expressing his understanding of the interconnectedness of the spiritual and worldly realms, Spencer employs a number of analogies or metaphors, from the circularity of the African American ring-shout to the return of the prodigal son.

This circularity, however, defines Spencer's argument as much as his subject, for he not only demands that the reader take a new theoretical approach to music, but also that the reader abandon the hermeneutic traditions that inform post-Enlightenment scholarship. He asks us to abandon the scientific rigor of anthropology and sociology, which he sees as Euro-cultural blinders that prevent a clear view of African-derived traditions. He also eschews philosophical or metaphysical approaches to music, which investigate only the surface manifestations of the phenomenon. Rather, Spencer relies on "field 3" (borrowing his terminology from musicologist David Burrows)—in which "re-searchers" must apply their own spirituality and subjectivity, their own reflexive understanding, to the study of music.

Spencer thus sets the ground rules for his essay, which preempt any criticism of his theomusicology from the standpoint of either social scientific methodology or philosophical consistency. He aims for neither. The ring-shout circularity of Spencer's argument is therefore couched within the circularity of his reflexive and subjective approach to the investigation of black music. For example, he bases his contention that religion or spirituality is the bedrock of all African American music on Paul Tillich's "theology of culture," which posits the underlying religiosity of all human endeavor. Yet if all of human culture is basically theological, then it naturally follows that all of human music is basically theological. There is no entry or exit from this circularity.

After arguing for the fundamental nature of both religion and rhythm in African American culture, Spencer devotes three chapters to the theomusicological investigation of black folk music, popular music, and classical music. In each case, he begins by taking apart previously held ideas about these musics. Spencer counters the view of Robert W. Gordon that African American spirituals did not speak of social liberation; he criticizes the opinions of early black editorialists who saw no redeeming qualities in the blues; and he attacks the position of early-twentieth-century intellectuals who saw African American classical music as a betrayal of the "primitive" qualities they enjoyed in black folk and popular musics.

Fair enough—but Spencer has succeeded in little more than demolishing straw men. The opinions of these writers hardly represent modern views. When Spencer attacks more contemporary scholars, he is on shakier ground. Thus, he criticizes Samuel Floyd Jr., who asserted that no one has taken an interdisciplinary approach to black music; Spencer claims his own theomusicology as the comprehensive approach that Floyd seeks. Yet Spencer misses Floyd's point that the study of black music would benefit from holistic approaches that place black music within a larger contextual framework. The subjectivity and single-mindedness of Spencer's theomusicology disallow the kind of multidisciplinarity that Floyd seeks, while Spencer himself proves to be more text based and performer based in his analyses than Floyd demands.

Spencer's book is in fact long on preliminary argument and short on actual theomusicological analysis. His main analysis in the three chapters on types of black music is what he terms "spiritual archeology." In essence, this methodology identifies the religious bases of secular music and musicians. Thus, Spencer shows the spiritual underpinnings of the trickster figure in the blues (thereby showing the sacred in this secular song form); he identifies spirituality in the "soul" music of African American popular culture; and he traces the inherent spiritual and religious beliefs that inform the works of classical composer William Grant Still. But these analyses target the obvious. Spencer's examples from folk and popular music are sparse, and seem to be chosen especially for their religious themes. For example, he chose "Preaching the Blues" songs sung by Robert Johnson and Bessie Smith, among others, for his spiritual archeology, when these songs obviously use religion as a metaphor. His argument would have been better served by showing the spirituality of blues that used only nonreligious tropes (perhaps Bo Carter's bawdy compositions). Likewise, it is easy to show the spiritual nature of Still, who was a spiritualist. Perhaps Duke Ellington's religiosity would have been a more convincing subject of Spencer's theories.

The problems with Spencer's study are manifold. Despite his claim of interdisciplinarity, many of the sources he most relies upon are either his own previous writings or those of his fellow theomusicologists. At times he veers toward a dangerous ethnocentrism, as when he claims that the hearts of African Americans, as a whole, "beat a little differently" from those of European Americans; if he is implying that blacks have an inherent rhythm, then he denies the heterogeneity of African America, and perhaps unwittingly plays into the hands of some very old and discredited views.

Spencer's circularity and unconvincing arguments, however, do not detract from a central and important tenet of his philosophy—the unity and interrelatedness of black musics, whether they are defined as sacred or secular. The interchange of music traditions across lines of belief is an important and necessary component of research into African American music, and Spencer helps this process along. His attempt, however, at a unified theory of black music based on religion is an error. Religion is certainly one of the pillars of human civilization—and all of culture might be viewed through a religious filter. But the same claim can be made for politics, economics, aesthetics, or psycho-social relations. All may be used as starting-points for the understanding of human culture.

By renouncing scientific and philosophical underpinnings for his study in favor of subjectivity, Spencer has perhaps defeated his purpose. A scholarly study, complete with citations to previous scholarship and based on the exposition and application of a theory, lies at the heart of post-Enlightenment, European-based interpretation. By choosing this form of exposition, Spencer has placed his message at cross purposes with his medium. He remedies this situation in a most innovative fashion, and it is the saving grace of the book. His prologue is a sermon that he gave at a small Episcopal church in Mississippi on the topic of the sacredness of the blues. In microcosm, Spencer's sermon is his entire argument, and in the form of a sermon, it contains all of the power that his scholarly exposition lacks.

In fact, the reflexive and subjective stance demanded by Spencer's theomusicology works best not as a scholarly endeavor but as a form of performance. The blues song proclaims itself in its performance, as does the spiritual or the classical piece. The circularity inherent in performances, wherein the singer and the work define themselves by "being," is a beneficial circularity. Spencer's sermon, like the music that he talks about, is a performance that needs no further elucidation. It is the theomusicology that Spencer seeks, and it serves him better than any form of scholarship.

Standing Before the Shouting Mob

Lenoir Chambers and Virginia's Massive
Resistance to Public-School Integration
By Alexander S. Leidholdt
University of Alabama Press, 1997
208 pp. Cloth, $29.95

Reviewed by **Carl Tobias**, professor of law at
the University of Montana and graduate of Petersburg,
Virginia, public schools and the University of Virginia
School of Law.

Alexander Leidholdt's *Standing Before the Shouting Mob* is primarily a biographical account of Lenoir Chambers, the editorial page editor of the *Norfolk Virginian-Pilot*. The book emphasizes the role that Chambers and the newspaper played in shaping public opinion during the half-decade period when Virginia practiced "massive resistance" to the desegregation of public schools. The closing and peaceful reopening of the Norfolk schools sounded the death knell for massive resistance in Virginia and undercut the state's leadership role in preventing integration across the South. Indeed, Norfolk was arguably the linchpin in the long, divisive struggle to implement the mandate of *Brown v. Board of Education*.

Perhaps the greatest contribution of *Standing Before the Shouting Mob* is its depiction of efforts to desegregate public schools in a specific locale, with particular reference to journalism's role in influencing public opinion. If the Commonwealth of Virginia was the leader of southern efforts to oppose desegregation, Norfolk was central to massive resistance in Virginia. Had peaceful integration proved difficult to achieve in this, the most politically progressive city in the state, desegregation might have been impossible in other communities.

Leidholdt carefully traces how Virginia's statewide political leaders, most prominently U.S. Senator Harry F. Byrd Sr. and Governor J. Lindsay Almond, formulated the policy of massive resistance. Readers learn that white politicians, who principally represented the Black Belt, forged a program aimed at preventing desegregation throughout the state. They were keenly aware that public-school integration anywhere in Virginia would eventually lead to desegregation across the Commonwealth and that integration would be achieved more easily in areas that had smaller African American populations or which enjoyed a more progressive political climate.

These statewide political leaders encouraged the state legislature to enact a series of statutes that essentially prevented desegregation by imposing insurmountable obstacles to requests made by African Americans who sought transfers to previously all-white schools. They required the closing of any public schools that did integrate and furnished tuition grants to attend private facilities for those pupils whose schools were closed.

Leidholdt focuses on the effect of this legislation in Norfolk. He examines the federal court litigation mandating that the Norfolk School Board admit African Americans to white schools, the governor's concomitant closing of those educational facilities, and subsequent litigation in federal and state courts that forced the schools' reopening. The author painstakingly details the comprehensive, careful efforts of Chambers and the *Virginian-Pilot* to educate the public about the desegregation controversy and to facilitate the dispute's peaceful resolution. Leidholdt draws thoroughly on Chambers's editorializing throughout the five-year period to illustrate the newspaper's impact on massive resistance.

Some of the best new material in the book is derived from Leidholdt's personal interviews with numerous participants in the desegregation dispute. Illustrative are discussions with Walter Hoffman, the federal judge who resolved much of the relevant litigation, and Chambers's colleagues at the newspaper. Leidholdt also shares keen insights into race relations in 1950s Norfolk and Virginia. For example, he finds that Chambers's editorializing was animated more by respect for the Constitution and the rule of law than for racial justice and fairness. In comparison, Leidholdt suggests that the white political leaders who articulated the notion of massive resistance were motivated more by concern for perpetuating their own political futures and white racial privilege than concern about state sovereignty.

Notwithstanding these important contributions of *Standing Before the Shouting Mob*, the author could have improved the book in certain ways. Although Leidholdt enhances our understanding of desegregation by focusing on a specific locale, his book is more a snapshot than a richly textured account of what happened in Norfolk. There is virtually no treatment of the African American political leadership in Norfolk or even of the efforts undertaken by the attorneys who successfully pursued the desegregation litigation. The mayor and the clerk of court, who played central roles in massive resistance, are effectively relegated to terse caricatures as tools of the powerful Byrd political machine. Perhaps most disconcerting is the colorless description of Chambers, the book's central figure. Most readers will come away from Leidholdt's work with little sense of what the newspaper editor was about.

Perhaps the clearest way to express these concerns with *Standing Before the Shouting Mob* is by contrasting the book to Davison Douglas's recent account of desegregation in Charlotte, North Carolina, titled *Reading, Writing and Race: The Desegregation of the Charlotte Schools* (see *Southern Cultures*, Spring 1998). Douglas paints an extraordinarily rich picture of the city, the participants in the controversy, the relevant litigation, the political machinations, the social fabric, and everyday life for African American and white citizens there. Ironically, Douglas's work affords a clear portrait of the *Charlotte Observer* and its editor, C. A. McKnight, and of the efforts undertaken by both, despite the fact that their roles are ancillary to the larger story of *Reading, Writing and Race.*

Standing Before the Shouting Mob has a few additional weaknesses. It succeeds more as an account of massive resistance or journalism history than as a full biography or legal history. Apart from the emphasis on Chambers and Norfolk, Leidholdt's book presents little material that is not already available, and often in greater detail, from other sources. I also found it difficult to follow the story line, the telling of which is occasionally disjointed—at times jarringly so. Nonetheless, the book does enhance our view of a regional, even national, struggle by exploring in detail how it unfolded in one city.

Author David T. Morgan

The New Crusades, the New Holy Land

Conflict in the Southern Baptist
Convention, 1969–1991
By David T. Morgan
The University of Alabama Press, 1996
246 pp. Paper, $24.95

Reviewed by **James L. Peacock**, Kenan
Professor of Anthropology, professor of comparative
literature, and Director of the University Center
for International Studies at the University of North
Carolina at Chapel Hill. He was president of the
American Anthropological Association from 1993 to
1995, and in 1995 was inducted into the American
Academy of Arts and Sciences. His fieldwork includes
studies in Indonesia.

As though following a kind of Gresham's law in the religious realm, fundamentalisms of various kinds have surged throughout the world at the expense of moderate or liberal perspectives. This is obviously true for Islam, reportedly true for Judaism, and apparent also for Christianity. In fact, the trend is of such concern to scholars of religion that some of us have joined together in a global study of fundamentalism, sponsored by the American Academy of Arts and Sciences and published in a series of volumes by the University of Chicago Press. In *The New Crusades, the New Holy Land*, David Morgan brings this global trend very close to home as he cogently details the ascendancy of fundamentalists and the purge of moderates and liberals in the Southern Baptist Convention during the period 1969 to 1991.

Among Morgan's Baptists, one does not encounter the physical violence of Iran or Afghanistan. We are a long way from clerics whipping women on the street when they display their ankles, for example. And it is worth remembering and appreciating the Baptists' relative civility (Morgan notes one incident of a prominent Baptist leader in Texas shooting another, but most violence is rhetorical). But the process of cultural control, thought control, and belief control has proceeded relentlessly, according to Morgan's account, and it is driven by narrow doctrine and a will to power. From reading this work, one concludes that the narrow and the dogmatic can and will prevail, especially when dogmatism in doctrine is supported by clever and ruthless pragmatism in ecclesiastical politics. Similar impressions are gleaned, of course, from recent trends in government, business, and education, where broader, more liberal views are falling victim to the know-nothings who act and scheme more vigorously than liberals and appeal to baser visions.

Such conclusions are not stated or even explicitly suggested by this book, which confines itself to a detailed narration of the recent rise of fundamentalism in the Southern Baptist Convention. Morgan identifies the founding catalyst of the rise of fundamentalism as M. O. Owens, pastor of Parkwood Baptist Church in Gastonia, North Carolina; Owens shaped both doctrine and organization in the early years. However, Morgan identifies as the leaders of the contemporary movement Judge Paul Pressler, the Princeton-educated Texan, and Paige Patterson, also a Texan. Pressler was the organizer, Patterson the theologian. Morgan details the maneuverings of Pressler, Patterson, and others in various arenas. The annual Southern Baptist conventions (vividly evoked in Will Campbell's novel *The Convention: A Parable*) are well described as sites of electioneering where fundamentalists usurped leadership. The seminaries and colleges or universities are a second arena of contention. Many seminaries—for example, "Southeastern" at Wake Forest, North Carolina—were purged of liberal faculty (some of whom have found refuge of sorts at such places as Duke University), while the purge failed at such institutions as Baylor, Furman, and Wake Forest Universities, which instead seceded from the Convention. Churches are a third arena: a few, such as Binkley Baptist in Chapel Hill and Pullen Baptist in Raleigh (both North Carolina) split with the Convention.

Readers who are not Southern Baptists but who live in the South will be familiar—just from hearsay and newspapers—with many of the institutions, events, and people mentioned in *The New Crusades, the New Holy Land* and may even recognize family names here and there (someone with my own name is reported to call moderates "rats and skunks"). But more significant, Morgan's account is masterful in drawing together in coherent and gripping narrative a history that most of us know only superficially, through bits and pieces. That history is based not only on documents but also on extensive interviews with virtually all of the important players alive today and on observation of major events such as the annual conventions.

As a nonexpert, I found Morgan's book excellent and disturbing. Although he writes from a liberal or moderate viewpoint, he appears to document soundly and carefully a situation that should disturb everyone of liberal or moderate perspective: namely, that here in America's largest Protestant denomination there has arisen, insidiously, a challenge to liberalism and moderation (of which, granted, there can be too much, as when it becomes, itself, a kind of fundamentalism). Even more dangerous, what has emerged is a doctrinal and institutional structure in which debate itself is expunged. Observing this process in more than simply scattered accounts over the years—indeed in this concentrated narration— should cause us to sit up and take notice.

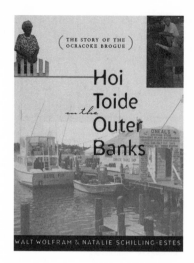

Hoi Toide on the Outer Banks

By Walt Wolfram and Natalie Schilling-Estes
University of North Carolina Press, 1997
Xiv + 165 pp. Cloth, $29.95; paper, $14.95

Reviewed by **Bruce Southard**, associate professor
of English at East Carolina University, whose research
interests focus on the dialects of Oklahoma and North
Carolina. His most recent publication, "Pronunciation
Variation in Eastern North Carolina," appears in
Language Variety in the South Revisited (University of
Alabama Press, 1997).

Separated from the mainland by some twenty miles, Ocracoke Island is the site of one of the oldest villages in the inhabited islands of North Carolina's Outer Banks. Founded in 1715, when the North Carolina Assembly passed a bill providing for settling and maintaining pilots at Ocracoke Inlet, an important but dangerous passageway through the barrier islands to the mainland ports, Ocracoke village for most of its history has been one of the most isolated communities on the Atlantic seaboard. Unlike other of the barrier islands connected to the mainland by bridges, even today Ocracoke is accessible only by ferry service. Indeed, until 1957, when the state first initiated ferry service across Hatteras Inlet to a newly constructed road leading thirteen miles to the village at the southern end of the island, the easiest means of gaining access to Ocracoke village was via a mail boat, which made a four-hour trip each morning from Atlantic, North Carolina. In 1960 ferry service was also inaugurated between Atlantic and Ocracoke.

The isolation of the inhabitants of the Outer Banks, and of Ocracoke in particular, has led to the development of a dialect of English that has attracted the attention of both language scholars and visitors to the Outer Banks since early in this century. In 1910, for example, Professor Collier Cobb delivered a lecture before an English literature class at Peace Institute in Raleigh that was later published as "Early English Survivals on Hatteras Island" (*North Carolina Booklet* 14 [October 1914]:91–99). Detailing word usage that he was able to trace back to Elizabethan equivalents, Professor Cobb ended his lecture by asserting that he had "noted greater changes in the speech of the people since the coming of the daily mail in motor boats, just ten years ago, than he had observed in the preceding thirty years, and the songs of the mothers and grandmothers are well nigh forgotten by the daughters."

The theme of losing a unique dialect is echoed in Robert Howren's "The Speech of Ocracoke, North Carolina (*American Speech* 37 [October 1962]:161–75). Howren noted in his first paragraph that "the motorcar and the ferryboat—a combination inevitably fatal to quaintness and picturesqueness—have brought perceptible changes to the Outer Banks. A good many linguistic archaisms and localisms have long since passed from usage, and inevitably further leveling will eventually result from close and continuous contact with the speech of the mainland." Howren's goal, then, was to record the speech of Ocracoke before it was replaced by "standard" speech. He concluded his article by noting that "the speech of the Outer Banks is obviously a fertile field for investigation, and one too-long neglected. It should be cultivated at once, for the Banks are becoming year by year less isolated and more susceptible to outside linguistic influence."

Hoi Toide on the Outer Banks, a work whose title is meant to reflect one of the most noticeable pronunciations of the Banks dialect, is the cultivated product of an intensive investigation of the language of Ocracoke conducted by Walt Wolfram, William C. Friday Professor of English at North Carolina State University, and Natalie Schilling-Estes, project coordinator for the North Carolina Language and Life Project (NCLLP). The NCLLP interviewed over seventy longtime Ocracoke residents, whose ages ranged from ten to ninety-one, recording well over one hundred hours of casual conversations that were fully transcribed phonetically by NCLLP staff and even subjected to spectrographic analysis with the aid of a Kay Elemetrics Computer Speech Lab. Yet *Hoi Toide on the Outer Banks* is not a dry academic treatise that details the fronting of back-rounded vowels or looks for the frequency of occurrence of vocabulary items characteristic of the Midland or Northern dialect areas.

Rather, the work makes such technical information accessible to the general reader, relying on common spelling conventions to indicate pronunciations, instead of expecting the reader to be familiar with the International Phonetic Alphabet and its various diacritics. Thus *hoi toide on the saind soide* represents "high tide on the sound side" and *feesh* is "fish." In like manner, the presentation of vocabulary centers on those ear- and eye-catching words unique to Ocracoke, but unfamiliar to non-*O'Cockers* (an island term for a native Ocracoker): *mommuck* (to bother someone); *doast* (sick, especially with the flu); or *quamish* (an upset stomach).

Wolfram and Schilling-Estes clearly conceive of this work as an opportunity to bring to public awareness the characteristics of a particularly interesting dialect, but at the same time to impart to the public a number of tenets: no dialect is inherently superior to another; groups of people use language, consciously or unconsciously, as a means of keeping themselves distinct from other groups; all dialects are governed by complex, rule-governed patterns that the speakers themselves may not be aware of; and language continually changes.

It is this last characteristic of language that clearly concerns Wolfram and Schilling-Estes, as it also concerned Cobb and Howren, for in their penultimate chapter they discuss the Ocracoke brogue as "an endangered dialect." Their task, clearly, is not to stand by and watch the dialect disappear as have so many endangered animals, plants, and languages. By creating "Save the Brogue" T-shirts and developing a curriculum on the dialect for use in the Ocracoke school, the NCLLP workers seek to raise public awareness of this particular language variety and, indirectly, any minority language form. Designed to educate both the tourists and, perhaps most important, the O'Cockers themselves, *Hoi Toide on the Outer Banks* is an informative survey of the Ocracoke brogue that presents the history of the dialect and its speakers; reviews its sounds, vocabulary, and grammatical constructions; places the dialect within the general picture of American dialects; and speaks eloquently of the need to celebrate and preserve the brogue.

Wolfram and Schilling-Estes write, "language is culture, and to lose a language is to diminish a culture." This book is an inspiring effort for those interested in the preservation of culture, for not only does it provide the most comprehensive record to date of the Ocracoke language and culture, but it will also serve as a guide for those who undertake comparable preservation projects. The NCLLP workers do not simply gather data for analysis; rather, they have a commitment to "work with the community to promote an understanding of and appreciation for the dialect." To help preserve the "hoi toide" dialect, they have actively involved the inhabitants of Ocracoke in the study of their own speech. They have prepared a documentary video, *The Ocracoke Brogue,* and have sought to educate the O'Cockers about the details of their own language to help them feel a sense of pride in its uniqueness. Through such efforts, the Ocracoke "hoi toide" may avoid becoming an ebb tide.

Soul Food

BY JOHN SHELTON REED

Lisa Howorth has observed that southerners can be distinguished by what goes into their mouths and what comes out of them. Many of the questions on the twice-yearly Southern Focus Poll deal with one or another of these aspects of the South. In the spring of 1995, 907 residents of the southern states and 506 other Americans were asked whether they had ever consumed a number of distinctively "southern" foods, a few nonsouthern specialties for comparison, and such nonfood comestibles as moonshine, chewing tobacco, and snuff. (The Fall 1992 poll had already asked about grits: those results were reported in the Summer 1995 issue of *Southern Cultures*.)

The data below document some expected differences, as well as reveal some surprising nondifferences:

Eat:	Often		Never or Don't Know	
	South	North	South	North
Grits**	26	5	34	61
Okra	40	11	22	48
Boiled peanuts	15	5	46	75
Moon Pie	15	4	37	66
Catfish	36	14	20	37
Sweet potato pie	22	14	24	41
Pork rind	15	9	38	49
Fried tomatoes	16	12	39	47
Chitlins	4	2	81	81
Moonshine	1	—	76	80
Chewing tobacco	*	*	77	80
Snuff	*	*	85	87
Vension	16	15	39	37
Caviar	2	2	71	68
Arugula	2	2	90	86
Lox	2	3	82	74
Kielbasa	10	17	60	40

*Question was "Have you ever [chewed tobacco/dipped snuff]?"

**From Fall 1992 Southern Focus Poll ("Often" is "a few times a month" or more).

The data below show patterns within the South for some of the items that show the greatest regional differences:

	Okra	Catfish	Moon Pie	Sweet potato pie	Boiled peanuts	Kiel- basa
Southern Total	78	80	63	76	54	40
Deep South	86	80	71	88	72	28
Peripheral South	76	80	60	71	47	45
Lived in South						
less than 10 years	59	75	55	73	41	59
more than 10 years	80	80	56	72	55	53
all my life	83	81	70	80	57	34
Residence at age 16						
South	82	80	68	78	55	34
border states	66	82	63	74	45	42
non-South	66	79	45	67	46	69
Considers self						
southerner	84	82	69	79	56	37
does not	61	72	54	66	44	50
Nonmetropolitan	78	78	65	74	52	32
Metropolitan	79	81	62	76	55	44
White	80	82	64	73	53	43
Black	71	70	63	97	51	24
Male	78	83	65	73	58	40
Female	79	78	61	78	50	40
18–24	55	80	67	66	50	22
25–44	77	80	66	73	53	46
45–64	90	82	67	82	57	44
65+	79	76	42	79	52	31
11th grade or less	69	72	63	79	53	17
High-school graduate	77	80	64	75	49	35
Some college	81	80	64	74	59	38
College graduate	82	82	63	76	54	55

Income						
less than $20,000	70	77	62	73	54	32
$20,000–$39,999	79	76	62	76	51	39
$40,000–$59,999	88	86	71	77	60	46
$60,000 +	81	84	58	77	54	52
Republican	80	84	62	76	53	42
Democrat	79	77	65	80	53	38
Independent	80	81	67	70	57	44
Other	78	68	63	74	41	37
Church attendance						
never	66	73	58	64	49	50
less than weekly	82	81	68	74	57	40
weekly	80	80	57	81	54	35
more than weekly	81	84	68	82	50	39

The Southern Focus Poll is a semiannual telephone survey conducted by the Institute for Research in Social Science at the University of North Carolina, Chapel Hill 27599-3355. Data can be obtained for further analysis from the Institute. The Institute's survey data holdings can be searched online at: www.irss.unc.edu:80/data_archive/pollsearch.html

Wie Geht's, Y'all?
German Influences in Southern Cooking

BY FRED R. REENSTJERNA

While a great deal has been made about Celtic and English influences in southern culture, less attention has been paid to other significant European influences. Most especially, German culinary traditions were established in several key regions of the South by the mid-1700s, and these traditions continue to this day.

German settlement in the eighteenth-century South was the result of English colonial policy in the Carolinas and Virginia. South Carolina planters lived in

Courtesy of the North Carolina Collection, University of North Carolina at Chapel Hill.

fear of Native American and slave uprisings, and they wanted colonies of white militiamen available on their borders. They devised a Township Plan, recruiting colonists from German Europe to settle in an arc ranging from along the Savannah River over through Columbia and down to Orangeburg, South Carolina.

Most of the townships failed, in part because they were put down in swampy landscapes bearing little resemblance to the homelands of German settlers. One settlement that did take hold, however, was Saxe Gotha Township. The region between the Broad and Saluda Rivers is known as the Dutch Fork even today, reflecting its German origins. Comprising modern Lexington County and Saluda County (and the land now under Lake Murray), this settlement took root as a center of evangelical Lutherans—and their food.

Take, for example, chicken and dumplings. This mainstay of mountain culture, which is actually served throughout the non-German South, is a stew of chicken and vegetables covered with a thick flour paste that is cooked by the steam of the boiling broth. In the Saxe Gotha region, by contrast, "dumplings" are flour noodles about two inches square. The region has become so homogenized since 1970 that food stores no longer carry dumplings in that size, but they did in my youth. I know this because my mother, once assigned to bring the dumplings to a family dinner and too busy to make a batch by hand, bought a package of prepared dumplings and sprinkled some flour over them to make them look homemade. Nobody knew the difference. Today, however, the only "extra-wide" noodles in food stores are barely an inch across.

These kinds of "dumplings" are only one German culinary tradition. Liver pudding, quite a distinct food from pork sausage, is another characteristic of Saxe Gotha. Its distinctly South Carolinian feature is that it combines rice with ground pork organ meats, mixed with red pepper and other seasonings, all stuffed into casing. Commercial liver pudding in food stores is pretty bland, but "real" pudding is available at Caughman's meat plant outlet ("The Meat'n Place") and Four Oaks Farm. Both of these places are within a mile of each other in Lexington County and are operated by old Saxe Gotha families (the Caughmans and the Mathiases).

But the most distinctive German food to come out of Saxe Gotha is liver nips. Clearly of Central-European heritage, liver nips are still cooked in central South Carolina. Basically, "nips" are a paste of ground beef liver, stew beef, eggs, and flour, spooned into boiling beef broth. Cutting into the paste with a spoon was referred to as "nipping" some of it off—hence liver nips. They are also called liver dumplings nowadays—an interesting reminder of the southern-style chicken and dumplings discussed above. As the nips cook, some of the material falls off into the beef broth, producing a kind of thick sauce (or a really lumpy gravy, if you're disrespectful).

Two critical elements in liver nips are the seasonings and the amount of flour. Nips are heavy on thyme and other herbs; cooking nips fill the kitchen with a heady, herbal, almost sausage-like aroma. The amount of flour is critical in final consistency, and recipes vary from family to family. Some people prefer a "tight" nip, made with lots of flour, while others prefer a looser nip. The finest nips ever, at least according to our family tradition, were made by Mrs. Clara Harmon. Regrettably, her grandson does not like liver nips, so that branch of the nip evolutionary tree has come to a dead end.

Liver nips are properly served with "mix bread" (or mixed bread), so named because the dough is mixed rather than kneaded. The central element of mix bread is cooked grits, which is mixed with flour and yeast and left to rise twice before baking. The ingredients cooked into mix bread yield a product with a tough crust and a spongy interior—ideal for sopping up the broth associated with liver nips.

Few commercial establishments serve chicken and German-style dumplings, and fewer still offer liver nips, but one place still serves both. Shealy's Restaurant in Leesville, South Carolina, maintains the traditional cuisine of old Saxe Gotha Parish in an all-you-can-eat, family-style buffet. The Shealy family began catering the Gilbert Peach Festival over thirty years ago, long before the suburbanization of Lexington County, and they have continued serving authentic food at their restaurant.

Recent (1997) menu modernization at Shealy's has included the addition of barbecued ribs to traditional (pulled-pork) barbecue, but the buffet still includes chicken and dumplings on occasion. Thursdays are liver-nip days, and you can tell from the turnout that not all Lexingtonians moved to the area within the past fifteen years (even though it may seem that way during rush hour on Highway 378). The wide expanse of family-style tables allows people to move among the seats, making the obligatory greetings to individuals in their ken (which usually means about 75 percent of the diners at any given moment).

Because Germans have been in the South for over 250 years, they have blended more completely into southern culture than, say, Germans in Pittsburgh or Detroit. Nonetheless, their unique culinary contributions to the diversity of southern cooking remain distinctive, to be recognized and enjoyed.

"Battle Songs of the Southern Class Struggle"

Songs of the Gastonia Textile Strike of 1929

BY PATRICK HUBER

The bitter hatred displayed by the capitalists and their spokesmen, the press, government and pulpit, against the Gastonia strikers, has imprinted itself so indelib[ly] in the hearts of the southern working class, that their children are singing folk songs that have arisen spontaneously from their struggles.
—*Daily Worker*, 26 July 1929

On 25 August 1929 Margaret Larkin attended an outdoor strike rally near Mount Holly, a textile-mill town eight miles northeast of Gastonia, North Carolina. A left-wing journalist from New York City, Larkin had come south that summer to cover the upcoming trial of sixteen members of the National Textile Workers Union (NTWU) accused of murdering Gastonia police chief Orville F. Aderholt. On this particular day, despite occasional showers, more than five hundred striking workers from several Gaston County textile mills had gathered at the all-day "speakin'" and barbecue. When Larkin arrived at the event, a union member named Ella May Wiggins was leading the assembled workers in a rousing rendition of "Chief Aderholt," a ballad she had composed about the police officer's death and the falsely-accused strikers' imprisonment. Wiggins was a "'slightly' woman," Larkin noted, "rather short and round," with "bobbed brown hair" and "lively brown eyes that had survived the early aging of the Southern working woman."

But Wiggins's ringing alto voice and the crowd's enthusiastic response to her songs made the deepest impression on the northern journalist. "She had a clear, true tone in her untaught voice, an unmodulated vibrancy that touches the emotions more nearly than the purer notes of trained singers," remarked Larkin. "Hundreds of workers" crowded around the speaker's platform, "their faces up-turned to the singer, their lips following the words":

> We're going to have a union all over the South,
> Where we can wear good clothing and live in a better house.
> Now we must stand together and to the boss reply,
> We'll never, no, we'll never let our union die.

"Many of the audience had heard it and learned it already; dozens more were memorizing it on the spot." Such songs, Larkin concluded, were "better than a hundred speeches," because they "would travel through the textile towns, telling better than speeches or leaflets of the people's faith in the union to give them a better life."

Margaret Larkin's colorful description of this union rally reveals the central role that protest songs played in the Gastonia textile strike of 1929. It also suggests the extraordinary effectiveness of singing as a means of political mobilization in that prolonged labor struggle. Although songs of social protest had deep roots in the American South, the Gastonia strike marked one of the first labor conflicts in the region that produced a large repertoire of protest songs written specifically for the occasion. Strikers composed literally dozens of protest songs that described the grim plight of cotton-mill workers, outlined the broader issues of the strike, and chronicled the major events of the conflict. Thanks primarily to the ballad-collecting efforts of Larkin and other sympathetic journalists, no fewer than fourteen of the Gastonia strike songs have survived. Taken together, these innovative songs illuminate the ways in which singing united strikers in public displays of union solidarity, expressed the shared grievances of the strikers, and revived flagging enthusiasm as the doomed strike dragged on. Such functions, of course, were crucial in sustaining the prolonged Gastonia strike amidst the brutally repressive campaign waged by the powerful combined forces of mill bosses, community leaders, national guardsmen, and local law enforcement officers.

The Gastonia protest songs actually emerged during a much larger, region-wide series of strikes unleashed by an economic depression in the southern textile industry. Throughout much of the 1920s textile manufacturers struggled to keep afloat amidst shrinking international markets, increased overseas competition, and soaring production costs at home. Under such deteriorating economic conditions, mill superintendents responded with drastic measures: laying off workers, slashing wages, installing new labor-saving machinery, and introducing new managerial practices. Chief among management's new shop-floor practices was the notorious "stretch-out," the name southern millhands used to describe the series of workload redistributions that not only often doubled the amount of work required of spinners and weavers but reduced their wages as well. By the late 1920s southern mill workers were overworked, underpaid, and stretched to the breaking point

Their anger and frustration erupted in a large-scale labor revolt. During the spring of 1929 a wave of textile strikes swept across the southern Piedmont, disrupting patterns of everyday industrial life in literally hundreds of textile-mill communities. The most famous strike that year occurred in Gastonia, North Carolina, a sprawling industrial city of 17,000 residents. Gaston County contained

An outdoor rally held during the textile workers' strike in Gastonia, North Carolina, 1929.
Courtesy of the Archives of Labor and Urban Affairs, Wayne State University.

more cotton mills than any other county in the South and the third most in the nation. Gastonia, its county seat, was one of the leading textile manufacturing centers in the South. There, the strike revolved around the Loray Mill, a massive brick factory, five stories high, which manufactured combed yarn and automobile tire cord fabric. With 2,200 workers, the mill, a subsidiary of the Manville-Jenckes Company of Rhode Island, was the largest textile plant in Gaston County.

Although only one of hundreds of Piedmont communities rocked by labor strife in 1929, Gastonia captured more national and international attention than any of the other conflicts. The small southern city made headlines around the world chiefly because of the participation of the recently founded NTWU, one of the dual unions of the Communist Party U.S.A., but also because of the intense

LABOR DEFENDER
JULY 1929   10¢
SMASH THE MURDER FRAME-UP
DEFEND GASTONIA STRIKERS!

THE 14 SOUTHERN
TEXTILE STRIKERS
SHALL NOT DIE!

Cover of the July 1929
Labor Defender *showing*
Fred Beale and others accused
of Aderholt's murder.
Courtesy of the Gaston County
Museum of Art & History.

bitterness and bloody violence that punctuated the five-and-a-half-month strike. The conflict began on April Fool's Day 1929, when 1,800 of the Loray Mill's 2,200 workers walked off their jobs. The NTWU, under the local leadership of a young Massachusetts Communist by the name of Fred E. Beal, promptly organized a union local and called a strike. Among other concessions, the strikers demanded a minimum $20 weekly wage, a forty-hour work week, union recognition, and an end to the hated "stretch-out." Soon, textile workers from other Gaston County mills joined the protest.

A few days after the strike began, North Carolina governor O. Max Gardner, himself a mill owner, sent five companies of national guardsmen to the city to protect mill property and to maintain order on the picket line. The city newspaper, the *Gastonia Gazette*, exacerbated tensions in the community with its inflammatory anti-Communist editorials. "Shall men and women of the type of Beal and associates, with their Bolshevik ideas, with their calls for violence and bloodshed, be permitted to remain in Gaston County [?]" the newspaper's incensed editor demanded. When the governor withdrew state troops, civic leaders organized a vigilante group called the "Committee of One Hundred" to patrol the strike zone. On 19 April the mob demolished the union's headquarters and relief

store. Three weeks later the Loray Mill superintendent evicted striking workers and their families from company-owned housing, and the union set up a tent colony a few blocks from the factory.

Over the next few months the violence escalated. On the night of 7 June, Police Chief Orville F. Aderholt was fatally wounded during a police raid on the evicted strikers' tent colony. Sixteen organizers and strikers, including Fred Beal, were arrested and charged with first-degree murder and conspiracy. On 9 September, after the first trial ended in a mistrial, a mob raided the rebuilt union headquarters and tent colony, kidnapped three organizers, and terrorized strikers and their families. Five days later, vigilantes ambushed a truckload of unarmed strikers en route to a union rally and shot and killed Ella May Wiggins, a single mother of five and one of the strike's most prolific balladeers. Soon afterwards, the Gastonia strike collapsed.

Protest songs and music played an integral role throughout most of the Gastonia textile strike. In part this resulted from the fact that singing complemented the industrial folkways of the striking workers, especially the middle-aged women who, according to one labor organizer, "knew any number of ballads, most of them rather mournful." But singing also constituted a key element of the NTWU's

Two women struggling with a state militia trooper during the textile workers strike in Gastonia, North Carolina, 1929. Courtesy of the Archives of Labor and Urban Affairs, Wayne State University.

calculated strategy for building a strong, viable union movement in the hostile, strike-busting atmosphere of the American South. Strike leader Fred Beal, a veteran of several New England textile strikes, had encouraged the workers to sing from the onset of the conflict. "From experience," he later wrote, "I knew the tremendous value of singing the right songs on a picket line. These workers knew none of the union's strike songs. To overcome this, I typed a number of copies of *Solidarity* and told them to sing it to the tune of *Glory, Glory Hallelujah* [*sic*]." Beal and his staff of chiefly northern and midwestern organizers also taught Gastonia strikers several other labor anthems, including such Industrial Workers of the World (IWW) standards as "Casey Jones—The Union Scab," "The Preacher and the Slave," and "The Tramp."

But the exchange of songs during the Gastonia strike was a reciprocal process that ran both ways. Northern union organizers introduced labor anthems and IWW songs to southern mill workers, but they, in turn, taught a whole host of traditional southern ballads and recorded hillbilly songs to the organizers. Vera Buch, the NTWU's deputy strike leader, left a brief but excellent description of the cultural exchanges that occurred time and again during the Gastonia strike. In her autobiography, *A Radical Life* (1977), Buch recalled how once when jailed for breaking an ordinance against picketing, a cell full of women organizers and strikers whiled away the hours talking, getting to know one another, and swapping songs: "We sang a lot: 'Solidarity Forever' and 'The Red Flag': 'Though cowards flinch and traitors sneer / We'll keep the red flag flying here.' The strikers sang their own beautiful plaintive ballads, 'Barbry [*sic*] Allen,' 'Red River Valley,' and many more." Mary Heaton Vorse, a labor journalist who later wrote a proletarian novel about the Gastonia conflict titled *Strike!* (1930), collected several traditional ballads and hillbilly songs that circulated among the strikers, including "Barbara Allen," "Birmingham Jail," "The Knoxville Girl," "The Lexington Murder," and "Waiting for a Train."

Despite the musical exchange, northern middle-class organizers and southern working-class strikers encountered one another in Gastonia across a vast cultural and class divide, one no doubt enlarged by the doctrinaire Marxist ideology of the Communist organizers. "You know," Vera Buch confided to Mary Heaton Vorse, "it's strange about these people. They are Americans like we are and yet our foreign workers in the North are much more comprehensible to us." Outside strike organizers and journalists almost without exception saw Gaston County mill workers as a premodern, backward people. The mill workers Vorse encountered, for instance, struck her as an archaic, tradition-bound "folk," very much out of step with the modern industrial South. "They do not belong to this century," she observed. "Their point of view toward the clan, their kin, society, their bosses, is of the seventeenth or eighteenth century." Margaret Larkin shared similar views. She described the local millhands as "mountain people, with the habits of peasants, . . . [who] are suddenly confronted with modern industrialism."

And the strike itself exposed cultural and ideological differences between outside organizers and local strikers, such as the heated controversy that raged in the NTWU local over "white chauvinism" and union integration. Music could also be a bone of contention. Fred Beal, for example, later confessed that "Solidarity Forever" might not have been the best choice to teach Gastonia strikers. The classic labor anthem, he later realized, employed the same tune as "John Brown's Body" and therefore "was perhaps somewhat inappropriate for Southerners." Outside strike leaders failed to comprehend fully the complicated intricacies of the southern striker's common working-class culture, and such cultural ignorance often brought the competing visions of the conflict into sharp relief. But despite such differences, strike leaders and rank-and-file unionists together were able to create a vibrant patchwork culture of events, music, and rituals that helped sustain the beleaguered union throughout the prolonged strike.

Perhaps the most remarkable feature of the Gastonia strike culture was the original protest songs that workers composed during the conflict. Such songs actually developed out of the cultural tensions that existed between organizers and strikers. Occasionally, the Gastonia strikers refused to sing "Solidarity Forever" and the union's other ponderous labor anthems in favor of their own familiar secular ballads and sacred hymns. More inspired workers made up their own simple, unpolished songs. Since protest songs were designed to generate mass participation and since it was much easier to compose new lyrics than new melodies, striking workers simply fitted new words to existing tunes. Russell D. Knight, for example, modeled "We Need You Most of All" on the popular "heart song," "I Love You the Best of All." Its opening stanza made a direct appeal:

> The time has come for our freedom
> We must stand up and fight
> The strike is on[,] boys[,] stick to it
> And we will win out all right.

Several organizers and journalists remarked on southern workers' penchant for composing their own protest songs. "A workers' string orchestra played songs written by the workers themselves," commented a correspondent for the *Daily Worker,* the Communist Party's newspaper, in his coverage of one of the NTWU's summer-time picnics. Communist editor Bill Dunne also took note of the strikers' musical creations he heard at a joint labor conference and legal defense rally in Bessemer City. "A remarkable feature of these two gatherings," he observed, "was the singing of union songs composed by the union members themselves and set to the crooning airs of the southern folk music. The southern class struggle is developing its own battle songs already." Margaret Larkin, herself an amateur folklorist, was keenly interested, as she wrote, in the "'Song Ballets' which had been 'posed' by various poet-singers. At first I thought that they must be parodies of songs their authors knew," she later confessed. "So I asked the singers to give me the original words in every case. I found that phrases from the originals or from other familiar ballads were sometimes incorporated into these, but that the heart of the song was always the author's own." Larkin predicted that the Gastonia strike songs "are destined to be the battle songs of the coming industrial struggle."

Among the strikers, children played an especially important role in composing new songs. "The children of the Gastonia strikers have put their words to tunes," the *Daily Worker* reported on 26 July, "and any evening in the tent colony you can hear them singing in typical 'blues' melody of the South." One of them, Odell Corley, an eleven-year-old spare hand, composed several strike songs, including

"Up in Old Loray" and "Come On You Scabs If You Want To Hear." She wrote new words for "Up in Old Loray," for instance, to the melody of the mournful ballad, "On Top of Old Smoky." Corley replaced, as one group of historians has pointed out, "the false-hearted lover with a crooked boss and the betrayed woman with a spirited striker." One particularly poetic stanza warned:

> The bosses will starve you,
> They'll tell you more lies
> Than there's crossties on the railroads,
> Or stars in the skies.

The August 1929 issue of the left-wing journal *New Masses* published another one of Corley's ballads, "Can I Sleep in Your Tent Tonight, Beal," a parody of "Can I Sleep in Your Barn Tonight, Mister," written from the perspective of a scabbing millhand who, cold and hungry, has a change of heart. One stanza goes:

> Manville-Jenckes has done us dirty,
> And he set us out on the ground.
> We are sorry we didn't join you
> When the rest went out and joined.

New Masses went so far as to dub young Corley "the 'poet laureate' of the strike." Another young Loray striker named Kermit Harden wrote "Union Boys," which he modeled on the Tin Pan Alley hit "Sonny Boy." One stanza promised:

> Manville Jencks [*sic*] betrays us, but the workers all stand by us,
> We still have the union, union boys.
> And when we get our high pay, we will never, never stray
> From our eight-hour day, union boys.

Although men and boys did compose a few strike songs, based on the sample of surviving songs women and teenage girls were the predominant creators of new protest ballads for the strike. They also participated in the textile strikes of 1929 in far "greater proportion than they worked in the mills." In Gastonia, as elsewhere across the southern Piedmont that spring and summer, labor conflict opened new public opportunities for women to serve in their union locals, perform strike committee work, recruit union members, administer strike funds, distribute relief supplies, walk picket lines, deliver speeches, and, of course, compose strike ballads. Ballad composing in particular accorded women a status and prestige in their communities usually unavailable to them under peaceful conditions.

Ballad composing also offered women and girls opportunities to speak out on issues of importance to them. And no issue figured more prominently in their songs than the plight of wage-earning mothers and their children. For example, Daisy McDonald, a Loray striker who supported a family of eleven on $12.90 a week, wrote "The Speakers Didn't Mind," a long ballad that chronicled the arrest of strike leaders, the terrorizing of strikers and their families, and the destruction of the tent colony. Two stanzas recounted:

> They arrested the men, left the women alone,
> To do the best they can;
> They tore down the tents, run them out in the woods,
> "If you starve we don't give a damn."
> Our poor little children they had no homes,
> They were left in the streets to roam;
> But the W.I.R. [Workers International Relief] put up more tents and said,
> "Children, come on back home."

By far the most famous grassroots balladeer of the Gastonia strike was Ella May Wiggins, a spinner at American Mill No. 2 in Bessemer City whom the Communist press referred to as "the songstress of working class revolt in the South." Deserted by her no-account husband, Wiggins struggled to raise her five surviving children on $9 a week. During the strike she reportedly composed more than twenty songs championing the union's cause, including "All Around the Jailhouse," "The Big Fat Boss and the Workers," "Chief Aderholt," and the now-famous "The Mill Mother's Song." And like the other women balladeers, Ella May Wiggins worked her concerns as a wage-earning mother into her songs. According to Margaret Larkin, she modeled her "song ballets," as she called them, on "old mountain ballads" that she had learned as a girl growing up in the Blue Ridge Mountains of western North Carolina.

Ella May Wiggins often performed her strike songs at mass meetings and union rallies throughout Gaston County. As Vera Buch recalled, "She would write little ballads about the strike, set them to some well-known ballad tune, and sing them from the platform in a rich alto voice. Her rather gaunt face would light up and soften as she sang; her hazel eyes would shine; she became for the moment beautiful." Fred Beal, in his autobiography *Proletarian Journey: New England, Gastonia, Moscow* (1937), remembered her as a central figure at the nightly mass meetings. "No evening passed," he later wrote,

> without getting a new song from our Ella May, the minstrel of our strike. She would stand somewhere in a corner, chewing tobacco or snuff and fumbling over notes of a new poem scribbled on the back of a union leaflet. Suddenly some one would call for her to sing and other voices would take up the suggestion. Then in a deep, resonant voice she would give a simple ballad. . . . The crowd would join in with an old refrain and Ella May would add verse after verse to her song. From these the singers would drift into spirituals or hymns and many a "praise-the-Lord" would resound through the quiet night.

Cover of an issue of the Labor Defender *commemorating Ella May Wiggins. Courtesy of the North Carolina Collection, University of North Carolina at Chapel Hill.*

Ella May Wiggins proved to be such an extraordinary ballad composer because she transformed her personal experiences into universal songs that spoke directly to other textile workers, especially mill mothers. "When Ella May sang, 'How it grieves the heart of a mother . . .' every woman in her audience did know, and responded to the common feeling," observed Larkin. "When she sang, 'We're going to have a union all over the South,' the strike meetings thrilled to the ring of militancy in her voice." Fellow strikers actually believed that the Loray Mill's gun thugs had singled her out for assassination because of her influential role as a strike balladeer and her unswerving dedication to the union. "The bosses hated Ella May," claimed one striker, "because she made up songs, and was always at the speakings."

Among the more than twenty strike songs Ella May Wiggins composed, the most famous was "The Mill Mother's Song," a beautiful blues ballad that Margaret Larkin called "that classic expression of a working mother's love." The song, in its entirety, goes:

Ella May Wiggins's children, photographed shortly after their mother's death during the textile workers' strike in Gastonia, North Carolina. Courtesy of the North Carolina Collection, University of North Carolina at Chapel Hill

We leave our home in the morning,
We kiss our children goodbye,
While we slave for the bosses
Our children scream and cry.

And when we draw our money
Our grocery bills to pay,
Not a cent to spend for clothing,
Not a cent to lay away.

And on that very evening,
Our little son will say:
"I need some shoes, dear mother,
And so does sister May."

How it grieves the heart of a mother,
You every one must know,
But we can't buy for our children,
Our wages are too low.

It is for our little children
That seems to us so dear,

But for us nor them, dear workers,
The bosses do not care.

But understand, all workers,
Our union they do fear,
Let's stand together, workers,
And have a union here.

Collectively, the Gastonia strike songs not only reveal the inner story of that famous labor conflict, they also shatter stereotypes of southern textile workers and illuminate the ways in which modernity shaped their lives and identities. The Gastonia strikers were not the backward, uprooted mountain folk depicted in the autobiographies, articles, and recollections of Communist organizers and left-wing journalists. By the mid-1920s affordable Model T automobiles and the powerful media of radios, Victrolas, and Hollywood motion pictures had broken down southern textile workers' social isolation and had initiated them into a modern mass culture of consumption.

Admittedly, some Gastonia balladeers did set their strike songs to "old mountain folk tunes," as Margaret Larkin and others claimed. But almost half of the surviving songs were modeled on current phonograph records. Kermit Harden composed "Union Boys," for instance, as a parody of "Sonny Boy," a million-selling hit record that pop crooner Al Jolson had performed in the "talkie" motion picture *Singing Fool* (Warner Brothers, 1928). Other balladeers favored the latest hillbilly releases. Ella May Wiggins modeled "All Around the Jailhouse" on one of hillbilly singing sensation Jimmie Rodgers's biggest selling recordings, "Waiting for a Train" (Victor, 1928), issued less than two months before the Gastonia strike began. "The Death of Floyd Collins," a topical ballad about a doomed Kentucky cave explorer, inspired her "Chief Aderholt." One of the former song's most popular versions, which sold around 300,000 copies, was recorded by Vernon Dalhart (Columbia, 1925). The other side of Dalhart's disc contained "Little Mary Phagan," another topical ballad about the 1913 murder of an Atlanta factory girl. Ella May relied on its tune for "The Mill Mother's Song." Thus, the Gastonia strike songs, with their selective incorporation of regional and national music, reflect southern mill workers' increased participation in the national mass media and consumer culture of the Roaring Twenties.

Although the Gastonia strike songs were ephemeral, chiefly concerned with specific personalities and events whose immediacy soon faded, a few of them achieved limited circulation outside the South. Not only were they enormously influential as protest song models for the emergent left-wing folksong movement of the late 1930s and early 1940s, they also reemerged in more mainstream circles at the height of McCarthy's anti-Communist crusade. Folklorist John Greenway published ten of the songs in *American Folksongs of Protest* (1953), a pioneering study of grassroots labor and political songs. In 1955, Greenway, himself a folk revival singer of some accomplishment, cut a version of Ella May Wiggins's "Chief Aderholt" for his album, *American Industrial Folksongs* (Riverside, 1955). One year later, Pete Seeger recorded her "The Mill Mother's Song" under the title of "Mill Mother's Lament" for his 1956 Folkways Records album, *American Industrial Ballads*. The Gastonia strike songs have also appeared in numerous song anthologies and labor pamphlets, including *Hard Hitting Songs for Hard-Hit People* (1967), *Working Women's Music: The Songs and Struggles of Women in the Cotton Mills, Textile Plants and Needle Trades* (1976), and *Let's Stand Together: The Story of Ella Mae [sic] Wiggins* (1979). By the time this last booklet was published, the words that Margaret Larkin had written nearly fifty years earlier about Ella May Wiggins's ballads finally rang true. "With all the hard, conscientious work that she did for the union and the strike," Larkin remarked in 1930 in observance of the one-year anniversary of the Gastonia balladeer's death, "she still had energy and militant spirit left over, and she poured it into her songs, which her fellow workers sang and the whole labor movement sings now."

What's it sound like?

No field recordings exist of the Gastonia strikers singing, but two of their strike-inspired songs, both of them written by Ella May Wiggins, have appeared on folk revival albums recorded after World War II:

John Greenway, *American Industrial Folksongs*, Riverside Records, RLP 12-607. Recorded in 1955, this collection of coal-mining and textile-mill songs contains a version of "Chief Aderholt."

Pete Seeger, *American Industrial Ballads*, Folkways Records, FH 5251. An album of similar labor and occupational songs, recorded in 1956, includes "Mill Mother's Lament."

Where can I read more about it?

John Greenway, *American Folksongs of Protest* (University of Pennsylvania Press, 1953). A pioneering study of grassroots protest songs that contains sections on the songs of the Gastonia strike (pp. 133–39) and of Ella May Wiggins (pp. 244–52).

Margaret Larkin, "Ella May's Songs," *The Nation* 129 (9 October 1929):382–83. One of Larkin's two important articles that helped to establish the historical legacy of the martyred Gastonia balladeer as a labor activist and song composer.

John A. Salmond, *Gastonia 1929: The Story of the Loray Mill Strike* (University of North Carolina Press, 1995). A recent history offering a detailed, blow-by-blow account of the strike, with much attention devoted to the strike songs but little historical analysis.

Not Forgotten

How I Spent My Summer Vacation

BY LAUREN F. WINNER

My students last summer had never heard of Jim Crow.

U.S. Government is not an area in which I can claim expertise, but when I applied for a summer job with Duke University's Talent Identification Program—a camp for academically gifted middle- and high-school students—someone in hiring thought my few years' study of American history and religion qualified me to serve as a teaching assistant for American Government: Practical Politics. A few weeks after receiving my college diploma, I arrived in Durham, armed with notebooks, *The Federalist Papers*, and all the youthful optimism and energy we twenty-year-olds are supposed to possess.

At the faculty and staff get-to-know-you barbecue, three days before the students arrived, I was munching on a hot dog when a young black woman grabbed my arm and introduced herself as Sarah,[1] the instructor for the government course. "I'm so glad you're here," Sarah said. "I have a syllabus for you, and I've just received the student roster. I think we need to pray about what to do with this bunch!"

Twelve of our fifteen students were boys. All hailed from the South: Florida, North Carolina, Georgia, and Texas. All sharp as a whip. All white. (Not coincidentally, it is a minimum score on the SAT, taken in the seventh grade, that identifies participants for the Talent Identification Program.) An admixture of private and public school kids. All from privileged backgrounds.

In fact, we began the class by discussing what power and privilege are, concluding that power is something that must be accessed, while privilege can be enjoyed unawares. We drew up a list of different privileges in American society— gender privilege, class privilege, race privilege, age privilege. Sarah said that in the black community, she, very fair-skinned, enjoyed complexion privilege, and that she and her boyfriend also enjoyed heterosexual privilege. "James and I can walk down the street, all lovey-dovey, holding hands and kissing, and people croon, 'Oh, how cute, two folks in love,' but if two men tried to do that, people would say, 'How disgusting.'" Our students grasped age privilege and volunteered myriad examples of being followed in stores because proprietors suspected all teens of shoplifting. However, Sarah and I realized we had failed to communicate something essential when a thirteen-year-old from Texas raised his hand and asked, "Is welfare a class privilege? Only people from one class can get it. I mean, my mom can't just walk down to the welfare office and pick up a check."

That was the first clue that something was wrong.

Our class spent a portion of its six-hour day covering current events. Each student read a newspaper and selected one story to write about in his journal; then we discussed the events of the day as a group. Once, Brad wrote about an article that described various congressional approaches to tax reform. In discussion that evening, we deliberated the proposal to abolish income taxes in favor of a national sales tax. "How would this affect taxpayers?" I asked, and was gratified when Walter immediately shot up his hand and explained how substituting sales tax for income tax would shift the burden of payment onto people in a low-income tax bracket. But fourteen of my fifteen students said that would be fine with them. I saw the opportunity for a brief history lesson (I was squeezing them in wherever I could), and burst into an impromptu lecture on the Populists and the development of graduated income taxes in America. In five minutes we surveyed inheritance taxes and the lottery, too. Save my tenth-grader from Atlanta, who explained that paying a flat 30 percent income tax would mean nothing to Bill Gates but that for a family "earning $10,000 a year, that 30 percent might mean the difference between homelessness and survival," all of my students erupted into calls for a flat tax and abolishment of inheritance taxes. "No random poor person is gonna get my father's money when he dies," said the son of a Florida factory owner. "Yeah, *I* deserve that money, and I don't think it should go to the government in taxes," echoed Walter. "It's not fair."

Other history lessons came later. When Sarah lectured on the presidency, she mentioned L.B.J., observing that his Texas origins made his pushing civil rights all the more interesting. Jeffrey, a Texan himself, raised his hand and said, "I don't see what him being from Texas has got to do with anything, because this Civil Rights Act that you just mentioned, you said it was passed in 1964, which was a century after the Civil War ended, so there hadn't been racism or slavery or any of that for a hundred years, and the South and the North weren't opposed anymore, so I don't see why him being from Texas is such a big deal."

"Well, Texas was a Jim Crow state," said Sarah.

"Who's Jim Crow?" asked another one of our students.

Sarah and I glanced at each other, unsure whether Roy was being serious. I asked how many people knew what Jim Crow was, and two students raised their hands. All but one of these kids had southern parents who had attended Jim Crow schools. When I asked them how many could tell me something about segregation other than "Rosa Parks"—hoping that perhaps they knew the substance if not the moniker—three kids added something about water fountains and *Driving Miss Daisy*. That night we had another history lecture, beginning with 1863 and Reconstruction.

It was, to be sure, a moment of "taking stock."

What was the point of teaching these kids David Mayhew's theory that congressmen are single-minded seekers of reelection, or Richard Neustadt's argument that presidents try to serve five different constituencies, if they knew nothing of the long history of segregation in the South? These kids observed Martin Luther King Day every year, but who did they think King was? What did they think the activists of the Civil Rights movement were moving against? Did they think civil rights workers were just uppity niggers making a fuss at some lunch counters? Just what, exactly, had my students learned about the past at their Georgian dinner tables from their Georgian parents, or in their Georgian schools? (I knew that two of my students had just taken a year of Texas history in their schools at home, and recalling earlier class discussions, it became clear that they had learned plenty about the Alamo and the glorious struggle for Texas independence, if nothing else.) We had been talking about Yellow Dog Democrats for two weeks, but it had not occurred to us to explain just why many white southerners would have voted for a mangy, smelly house pet sooner than a Republican. We had taken them to the North Carolina legislature, and Dan Blue, former Speaker of the N.C. House, had spoken to them for an hour. I don't know what they thought it meant when I told them that Speaker Blue was the highest ranking African American political official in the state since Reconstruction.

I do understand, however, why most of my students were vociferously opposed to affirmative action. If I thought racism had ended 130 years ago with the signing of the Emancipation Proclamation, I might look askance at affirmative action myself. When we debated affirmative action in class, the students—understandably—most wanted to talk about college admissions. Their consensus was that special admission standards were okay for athletes, state residents, and children of alumni, but not for women or black people. One student wrote that affirmative action is a "racist, sexist system aimed at giving some underqualified individuals advantages they do not deserve." (Like many Americans, my students cast much of their political discussion in terms of who is deserving: I doubt that any of them would advocate abolishing free-lunch programs in grammar schools because fifth-graders are "undeserving.") The same student opined that "this racist and sexist system, goes directly against the American ideals of equality. . . . Affirmative action is a social cancer that needs to be destroyed before its evil seed can spread." Beneath the purple prose of an impassioned eighth-grader stands a perspective that should not be dismissed as mere child's play.

When I told the camp director about my students' ignorance of segregation, he (a teacher of advanced placement U.S. history at a private school in Tulsa) replied cavalierly, "Well, yeah, what did you expect?" I reckon I expected these kids—supposedly our best and brightest, who attend fine schools and have, as my mother would say, "every advantage"—to know about segregation. Naive, apparently.

If asked on a test, my students could now spit out two-sentence descriptions of Reconstruction and segregation. But they still failed to grasp the meaning of the Civil Rights movement, or of any protest movement at all. A constant refrain in class was that people ought not criticize America. "These people shouldn't sit around complaining about things while they're busy enjoying all the privileges of living in America. If they don't like it, they should just leave," said Jason. "What about those citizens who don't enjoy all the privileges of being an American?" I queried. "Who would that be?" asked one student. "Everybody gets to use the roads and stuff." Wonderful, I thought. While you're attending your posh private school and swimming at your country club and living in an eight-bedroom house, the rest of the folks get to use the roads.

There was more than a bit of cognitive dissonance in it all. Our class devoted one day to politics and popular culture. We watched clips of *Jungle Fever, Glory*, and *The Grapes of Wrath*, and the students brought in stacks of CDs so we could dissect the political messages in their favorite music. These kids, who knew nothing about segregation, appeared in class armed with highly nationalist black rap. One student played Nas's "If I Ruled the World (Imagine That)": "I'll open every cell in Attica/and send them all to Africa." Walter chose a song by Goodie Mob: "Yeah, it's true, Uncle Sam wants you to be a devil too / See, he's jealous 'cause his skin is a curse but what's worse / Is if I put it in a verse y'all will listen to some bullshit first / We ain't natural born killas, we are a spiritual people / God's chosen few. . . . / Goodie Mob means, 'The Good Die Mostly Over Bullshit' / You take away the 'O' and it will let you know / 'God is Every Man of Blackness.'" As I had wondered what the students thought Martin Luther King Day was about, so too I wondered what they thought these lyrics meant, and why they chose these particular tunes to accompany them in their cars as they used "the roads and stuff."

In my classroom, I witnessed the formation of a historical consciousness. As Eric Hobsbawm once noted, forgetting is as intrinsic to historical memory as remembering—and it was the forgetting that was outlined in clear relief last summer.

NOTES

1. All names of individuals mentioned in this essay have been changed.

About the Contributors & Editors

Louise Boyle is a life-long resident of Ithaca, New York, and a graduate of Vassar College. After studying photographic techniques in New York City, she photographed coal miners in Pennsylvania for *The Survey Graphic*. In 1937 she, along with social historian Priscilla Smith Robertson, lived for ten days in Myrtle Lawrence's home in Colt, Arkansas. The photographs here were taken with a Leica camera and are part of a larger collection to be published in book form by Elizabeth Payne.

Gavin James Campbell, music editor for *Southern Cultures*, is a doctoral student in history at the University of North Carolina at Chapel Hill. His dissertation topic is Atlanta's musical life in the early twentieth century.

Born and raised in the foothills of the Virginia Blue Ridge, **Michael Chitwood** is a freelance writer living in Chapel Hill, North Carolina. His poetry and fiction have appeared in *Poetry, The Southern Review, Threepenny Review, Virginia Quarterly Review, Field*, and numerous other publications. Ohio Review Books has published two books of his poetry—*Salt Works* (1992) and *Whet* (1995). His third book, *The Weave Room*, has been published by the University of Chicago Press in the Phoenix Poets series (1998). A book of his essays will also be published by Down Home Press in 1998. He is a regular commentator for WUNC-FM and a columnist for *The Independent* in Durham, North Carolina.

Patrick Huber is a graduate student in U.S. southern history at the University of North Carolina at Chapel Hill. His dissertation focuses on the social history of hillbilly music in the industrial upland South before World War II.

James L. Leloudis is associate professor of history at the University of North Carolina at Chapel Hill. Leloudis is coauthor of *Like a Family: The Making of a Southern Cotton Mill World* and author of *Schooling the New South: Pedagogy, Self, and Society in North Carolina, 1880–1920*. He is coeditor for reviews for *Southern Cultures*.

Jerry Leath Mills served from 1965 until his retirement in 1997 on the faculty at the University of North Carolina at Chapel Hill, where he was professor of English, editor of *Studies in Philology*, and an associate editor of *The Southern Literary Journal*. He is currently visiting professor of English at East Carolina University and coeditor for reviews for *Southern Cultures*.

Elizabeth Anne Payne is professor of history at the University of Mississippi, where she is also director of the McDonnell-Barksdale Honors College. She is the author of *Reform, Labor, and Feminism: Margaret Dreier Robins and the Women's Trade Union League*, as well as numerous articles in women's history. Professor Payne learned of Ms. Boyle's photographs and Arkansas visit while researching the history of the Southern Tenant Farmers' Union.

Robert M. S. McDonald is a Ph.D. candidate in history at the University of North Carolina at Chapel Hill. He is currently working on a study of Thomas Jefferson's public image, 1776–1826.

Celeste Ray is visiting professor of anthropology at Appalachian State University in North Carolina. She has trained in archaeology at the universities of Florida and Washington, the University College Galway in Ireland, and the University of Edinburgh in Scotland, where she researched Scottish national identity and the public presentation of battlefield landscapes. She became interested in Scottish American culture while completing her doctorate at the University of North Carolina at Chapel Hill. Her dissertation, "Scottish-American Heritage: Celebration and Community in North Carolina," is currently under revision for publication.

John Shelton Reed is William Rand Kenan Jr. Professor of Sociology and director of the Institute for Research in Social Science at the University of North Carolina at Chapel Hill. Among his recent books is *1001 Things Everyone Should Know About the South*, written with Dale Volberg Reed. He is coeditor of *Southern Cultures*.

Fred R. Reenstjerna, research librarian at the Douglas County Museum of History and Natural History in Roseburg, Oregon, grew up in Lexington, South Carolina. He was a regular visitor at the Kleckly Reunion, as well as at Lutheran church dinners and Homecoming picnics throughout the old Saxe Gotha township. A graduate of the College of Charleston, he earned graduate degrees at the University of Maryland, Lynchburg College, and West Virginia University. He coauthored "The Moving People: Ulster Traditions in the States of Jefferson and Franklin," which examines the continuity of Northern Irish political traditions from historical Eastern Mountain culture to contemporary Southwestern Oregon social issues.

Harry L. Watson is professor of history at the University of North Carolina at Chapel Hill. His most recent publication is *Liberty and Power: The Politics of Jacksonian America*. He is also coeditor of *Southern Cultures*.

Lauren F. Winner hails from Asheville, North Carolina. She studies history at the University of Cambridge, England, and is at work, with Randall Balmer, on a book about contemporary American evangelicalism.

North CAROLINA

Come Shouting to Zion

African American Protestantism in the American South and British Caribbean to 1830

SYLVIA R. FREY AND BETTY WOOD

"Provides insight into one of the great transitions in the history of the Americas. It is a work of originality, power, and significance."—Ira Berlin, University of Maryland at College Park
304 pp. $49.95 cloth / $16.95 paper

Exchanging Our Country Marks

The Transformation of African Identities in the Colonial and Antebellum South

MICHAEL A. GOMEZ

"This very important book deepens our knowledge about the major African ethnic groups important to the cultural formation of the United States . . . and reframes the discourse on African American cultures."—Gwendolyn Midlo Hall, Rutgers University
384 pp. $45 cloth / $18.95 paper

A Separate Canaan

The Making of an Afro-Moravian World in North Carolina, 1763–1840

JON F. SENSBACH

"An extraordinary story, brilliantly told."—Ira Berlin, University of Maryland at College Park
"A poignant case study of religious accommodation to social and economic forces."—Albert J. Raboteau, Princeton University
368 pp. $45 cloth / $17.95 paper
Published for the Omohundro Institute of Early American History & Culture, Williamsburg, Va.

NEW IN PAPER
Southern Cross

The Beginnings of the Bible Belt

CHRISTINE LEIGH HEYRMAN

"An extraordinarily rich exploration of the first hundred years of evangelical faith in the South. . . . Beautifully written."—Charles B. Dew, *New York Times Book Review*
352 pp. $16.95 paper

The Temptation

Edgar Tolson and the Genesis of Twentieth-Century Folk Art

JULIA S. ARDERY

"[This] account of the life of Kentucky woodcarver [Tolson]. . . . reveals the anguish, achievement, and triumph of a type of art . . . often cloaked in a garment of sweet innocence."
—John Michael Vlach, author of *Plain Painters*
376 pp., 7 x 10,
10 color / 77 b&w illus.
$45 cloth / $19.95 paper

COURTESY OF ESTELLE E. FRIEDMAN

A Paul Green Reader

EDITED WITH AN INTRODUCTION BY LAURENCE G. AVERY

"At last we have a valuable single volume which acquaints new readers with [Green's] work. . . . Another brilliant achievement."—John Ehle
384 pp. $39.95 cloth / $17.95 paper
Chapel Hill Books

We Mean to Be Counted

White Women and Politics in Antebellum Virginia

ELIZABETH R. VARON

"Invests antebellum southern white elite and middle-class women with a rich and complex political history."—Jane S. De Hart, University of California, Santa Barbara
248 pp. $45 cloth / $16.95 paper
Gender and American Culture
1995 Lerner-Scott Prize, OAH

NEW IN PAPER
Reconstructing the Household

Families, Sex, and the Law in the Nineteenth-Century South

PETER W. BARDAGLIO

"A model for future studies of the southern household."—*Southern Quarterly*
"Masterful."—*Georgia Historical Quarterly*
384 pp. $16.95 paper
Studies in Legal History
1996 James A. Rawley Prize, OAH

Quilts, Coverlets, & Counterpanes

Bedcoverings from the Museum of Early Southern Decorative Arts and Old Salem Collections

PAULA W. LOCKLAIR

Artistic expression in everyday textiles from 18th- and 19th-century America.
72 pp., 8½ x 11, 62 color / 5 b&w photos $16.95 pa
Distributed for Old Salem, Inc., Winston-Salem, N.C.

at bookstores or by toll-free order

The University of North Carolina Press

Chapel Hill • Phone (800) 848-6224, Fax (800) 272-6817 • http://sunsite.unc.edu/uncpress/

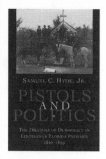

MISSISSIPPI QUARTERLY

MISSISSIPPI QUARTERLY
MISSISSIPPI QUARTERLY

Special Section
Eudora Welty
Fall 1997
Guest Editor: Albert J. Devlin, University of
Missouri

Suzan Harrison,
"It's Still a Free Country": Constructing
Race, Identity, and History in Eudora
Welty's "Where Is the Voice Coming
From?"

Michael Kreyling,
History and Imagination:
Writing "The Winds"

Ann Romines,
Reading the Cakes: *Delta
Wedding* and the Texts of
Southern Women's
Culture

Dawn Trouard,
Welty's Anti-Ode to
Nightingales: Gabriella's
Southern Passage

Suzanne Marrs,
Place and the Displaced
in Eudora Welty's *The
Bride of the Innisfallen*

Peter Schmidt,
On Optimists' Sons and Daughters:
Eudora Welty's *The Optimist's
Daughter* and Peter Taylor's *A
Summons to Memphis*

**Peggy Whitman
Prenshaw,**
The Political Thought of
Eudora Welty.

Susan V. Donaldson,
Making a Spectacle:
Welty, Faulkner, and
Southern Gothic

Noel Polk,
Welty, Hawthorne, and
Poe: Men of the Crowd
and the Landscape of
Alienation

Barbara Ladd,
Welty Studies:1987-1997

PAST SPECIAL ISSUES

Fall 1995
TENNESSEE WILLIAMS
*Guest Editor: Philip C. Kolin,
University of Southern Mississippi*

Spring 1996
ELLEN GLASGOW
*Guest Editor: E. Stanly Godbold,
Mississippi State University*

Spring 1997
RICHARD WRIGHT
*Guest Editors: Jack B. Moore,
University of South Florida
Michel Fabre, Université de la
Sorbonne Nouvelle*

Mississippi State
UNIVERSITY

MISSISSIPPI QUARTERLY

Special Issue
Prices Vary

Robert L. Phillips, Jr., Editor
Post Office Box 5272
Mississippi State, MS 39762-5272

Single Issues

$15 a year in the United States, $18 a year in Canada & Mexico, and $20 a year in other countries

V
Q
R

THE VIRGINIA QUARTERLY REVIEW

A National Journal of Literature and Discussion

SPRING 1998   *Volume 74, Number 2*

FIVE DOLLARS

Some of our good writers.

Jeff Baker
Brad Barkley
Richard Bausch
Maudy Benz
Roy Blount, Jr.
Blanche McCrary Boyd
Rick Bragg
Wendy Brenner
Larry Brown
Jack Butler
Will D. Campbell
Rosanne Cash
Fred Chappell
Michael Chitwood
Andrei Codrescu
Dennis Covington
Harry Crews
Hal Crowther
Guy Davenport
Tony Earley
Clyde Edgerton
William Faulkner
Richard Ford
Ellen Gilchrist
John Grisham
Peter Guralnick

Barry Hannah
Steven Harvey
John Hester
Fred Hobson
John Holman
Mary Hood
Andrew Hudgins
Zora Neale Hurston
Madison Jones
Donald Kartiganer
James Kilgo
Nanci Kincaid
Florence King
Beverly Lowry
Charles Marsh
Jill McCorkle
Elizabeth McCracken
Carson McCullers
Bill McKibben
Tim McLaurin
Thomas McNamee
Willie Morris
Jane Mullen
Lewis Nordan
Chris Offutt
Tom Paine

Robert Palmer
Tom Piazza
Jimmy Pitts
Padgett Powell
Sister Helen Prejean
Julia Reed
John Shelton Reed
Mark Richard
Diane Roberts
Louis D. Rubin, Jr.
John Fergus Ryan
Donald Secreast
Cynthia Shearer
Lee Smith
June Spence
Elizabeth Spencer
Donna Tartt
Clifton L. Taulbert
John Updike
Steve Vineberg
Brad Watson
Eudora Welty
Bailey White
Lynna Williams
Charles Wright
Steve Yarbrough

the Oxford American

"THE SOUTHERN MAGAZINE OF GOOD WRITING"

For a six-issue, one-year subscription, send $19.95 to:
The Oxford American / P.O. Box 1156
Oxford, Mississippi 38655-1156
or call toll-free 1-800-269-6926

The Sewanee Review

Winter 1998

American Poetry in This Century—Featuring a superb forum on Robert Frost, this issue includes essays on John Haines, Ezra Pound, Gary Snyder, William Stafford, Wallace Stevens, Allen Tate, James Wright, and others • two studies of meter • a witty view of the state of contemporary poetry • a goodly batch of new poems opening with a long one by Neal Bowers • and a beautifully crafted story by Phil Condon.

Spring 1998

Irish Letters Today—Given wholly to the literature of Ireland, this issue includes stories by Ann Chidester, William Trevor, and others • poetry by various hands in the United States and Ireland • familiar essays • and critical essays and reviews ranging over various aspects of contemporary Irish fiction and poetry, with emphasis on such writers as John Banville, Eavan Boland, Seamus Heaney, Thomas Kinsella, Bernard MacLaverty, Derek Mahon, and Edna O'Brien.

THE SEWANEE REVIEW $18 ONE YEAR
735 UNIVERSITY AVENUE $32 TWO YEARS
SEWANEE, TENNESSEE 37383-1000 $45 THREE YEARS

Transforming the Appalachian Countryside

Railroads, Deforestation, and Social Change in West Virginia, 1880–1920

RONALD L. LEWIS

"Lewis unravels the complex legal, social, and economic relationships that led to the destruction of West Virginia's forests. This is, to date, the most complete study of the impact of humans and their institutions on the Appalachian environment."—Timothy Silver, Appalachian State University

368 pp. $49.95 cloth / $18.95 paper

AVAILABLE SEPTEMBER
Selling Tradition

Appalachia & the Construction of an American Folk, 1930–40

JANE S. BECKER

"Fills a major need in cultural and regional studies. . . . Illuminates a pivotal . . . aspect of the cultural politics of the 1930s."
—David Whisnant, author of *All That Is Native & Fine*
"Demonstrates that as much as we would like to think otherwise, the Arts and Crafts movement relied on the creation of something like a sweatshop, now relocated into southern mountain homes."—Roger D. Abrahams, University of Pennsylvania

Approx. 360 pp., 37 illus.
$55 cloth / $18.95 paper

NEW IN PAPER
Reconstructing the Household

Families, Sex, and the Law in the Nineteenth-Century South

PETER W. BARDAGLIO

"A model for future studies of the southern household."—*Southern Quarterly*
"A signal contribution to legal history, the history of the family, and the study of southern race relations."—*Journal of Social Hist.*
"Masterful."—*Georgia Historical Quarterly*

384 pp. $16.95 paper
Studies in Legal History
1996 JAMES A. RAWLEY PRIZE

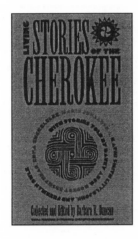

Living Stories of the Cherokee

COLLECTED AND EDITED BY BARBARA R. DUNCAN, WITH STORIES TOLD BY DAVEY ARCH, ROBERT BUSHYHEAD, EDNA CHEKELELEE, MARIE JUNALUSKA, KATHI SMITH LITTLEJOHN, & FREEMAN OWLE

"Through the years these legends have grown and changed and become contemporary with Cherokee people. . . . The critical message is that these stories continue."—from the foreword by Joyce Conseen Dugan, Principal Chief, Eastern Band of Cherokee Indians

Approx. 288 pp. $29.95 cloth / $15.95 paper

An Outer Banks Reader

SELECTED AND EDITED BY DAVID STICK

More than 60 selections from four centuries of the best writing about North Carolina's barrier islands. "[Stick's] exciting literary tribute to the place he knows so well and loves so much. A book as bracing as an ocean breeze."—Roy Parker Jr., contributing editor, *Fayetteville Observer-Times*
"An essential volume to every shelf of North Carolina history. . . . So interesting I couldn't stop reading."
—William Friday

336 pp. $29.95 cloth / $16.95 paper

at bookstores or by toll-free order

THE UNIVERSITY OF NORTH CAROLINA PRESS

Chapel Hill • Phone (800) 848-6224, Fax (800) 272-6817 • http://sunsite.unc.edu/uncpress/

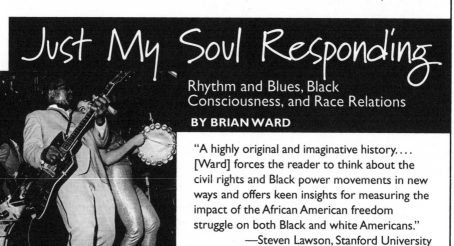